Canadian Gardening's
GREAT IDEAS
for the GARDEN

By LIZ PRIMEAU and THE EDITORS of CANADIAN GARDENING MAGAZINE
Consultants TREVOR and BRENDA COLE, FRANK KERSHAW

A FENN PUBLISHING COMPANY / MADISON PRESS BOOK

CANADIAN GARDENING'S

GREAT IDEAS
for the GARDEN

ISBN 1-55168-286-9

A FENN PUBLISHING COMPANY/
MADISON PRESS BOOK

First Published in 2005

FENN PUBLISHING COMPANY LTD.
Bolton, Ontario, Canada

Distributed in Canada by
H. B. FENN AND COMPANY LTD.
Bolton, Ontario, Canada, L7E 1W2

www.hbfenn.com

Produced by

MADISON PRESS BOOKS
1000 Yonge Street, Suite 200
Toronto, Ontario, Canada
M4W 2K2

Printed in Singapore

Contents

Introduction

It's a standing joke among gardeners that a visitor never chooses the right moment to "come and see the garden!" It's either over the hill (you really should have been here a couple of weeks ago, when the perennial border was at its peak) or it's not quite ready (if you could just come by in a few days, when the roses and the early lilies hit their stride...).

The truth is that gardens are seldom ready, and they're never finished. They evolve and change as the landscape does — influenced by nature, and guided by the hand of a gardener who is always in search of new ideas for creating the perfect garden.

And over 100 innovative and lavishly illustrated ideas are what we bring you in *Canadian Gardening's Great Ideas for the Garden*, one of the first titles in our exciting new series of gardening books written especially for Canadian gardeners. It's chock-full of inspiration — from creative ways to add style to a functional pathway, to arbors and pergolas both classic and casual, and bold new ways to use plants to best effect in your garden. Of course, you'll also find dozens of the practical how-to tips *Canadian Gardening* magazine is known for.

Wherever you live in Canada, we're confident you'll refer to *Great Ideas for the Garden* again and again for easy and creative ways to add to the beauty of your garden.

Liz Primeau
Editor, Canadian Gardening
Magazine

CHAPTER ONE

FENCES & GATES

*F*ences are an
important, but often overlooked, part of
any garden design. They lend form,
color and texture to a garden, set up an
interesting play of light and shadow, and
act as a backdrop for imaginative plantings
of shrubs, flowers and vines. Mysterious
and inviting at the same time,
they hint at the magic of the garden
and the private space beyond.

*In a lovely tribute to the Victorian gardens of yesterday,
fragrant roses and clematis embroider the arch
of an elegant wrought-iron gate. A tightly laid brick
path underscores the formality of the setting and echoes the
architectural style and materials of the house.*

A Fence is Never *just a* Fence

Much of the success of a fence design lies in the choice and use of materials.

Depending on where you place it or what materials you use, a fence can boldly hold the outside world at bay, screen a private corner of the garden, hide an unsightly view or create a number of outdoor rooms draped in climbing vines. It can be high, wide and solid, blocking the view completely and assuring privacy, or it can be airy and open, offering a tantalizing glimpse of the garden inside. Even a low fence can create a sense of enclosure and personal space simply by defining a boundary.

Here are some creative ways to give yourself a fence with style. Remember to choose a design that complements both the style of the garden and the architecture of the house or other nearby structure — then add the finishing touches that make it uniquely yours.

Fence Finery

🌺 Choose interesting fence posts to finish off a simple structure and to frame the garden gate. Add mouldings, ornamental finials or capping details that echo the architectural style of the house.

🌺 Make a traditional picket fence and gate more appealing by varying the spacing and height of rails and pickets.

🌺 Add height to a fence with espaliered trees (see p. 62) or with vines trained on wires installed horizontally above the top of the fence. The effect is both pretty — and private!

🌺 Include elegantly arched spaces over a gate to offer an enticing glimpse into the garden and to support a colorful vine or fragrant rose.

🌺 Cover a plain fence with lattice to give it presence. For greater effect, stain the whole structure to complement your planting scheme and add climbing roses, clematis or lush foliage vines.

🌺 Break the monotony of a closed fence by creating strategically placed openings to reveal the space beyond. Embellish with arches, peepholes or decorative hardware.

🌺 Set a panel of stained or frosted glass or decorative tiles into a solid privacy fence to provide a focal point and expand the visual dimensions of the enclosure.

🌺 Employ a little trickery to charm and delight — position a window in a fence with a trompe l'oeil view or a mirror to suggest acres beyond.

🌺 Stretch woven reed or bamboo across a frame for a delicate effect that allows air circulation and enhances the serenity of gardens with an Oriental style.

PRETTY PICKETS

Decorative finials atop the fence posts transform a simple country fence (above) into an elegant architectural statement. Note the gentle curving of the top rails. A purple wash of *Clematis* X *jackmanii* adds both color and contrast to the clean lines of the fence and the clipped cedar hedge beyond.

Like icing on a cake, climbing roses decorate the arrowhead pickets of this pretty fence (right) and provide a pleasing framework for the formal beds beyond. The owner has turned an otherwise wasted and difficult-to-mow space on the street side of the fence to advantage by creating an informal flower border in front.

ROSES *on the* RISE

The rose-covered fences, trellises and archways that Canadian gardeners once only dreamed of are now a beautiful reality in gardens across much of the country — thanks to some of the roses in the Explorer series, as well as other hardy varieties that have been created especially for northern climates.

❦ Vigorous, disease-resistant and hardy to Zone 4, Explorer roses were first developed at the Central Experimental Farm in Ottawa in the early 1960s; the program is now in L'Assomption, Quebec.

❦ Although most Explorers are bush or shrub types, the series also includes taller, long-shooted varieties that can be grown as climbers. Among the best of these are 'John Cabot' (deep orchid-pink double blooms), 'Henry Kelsey' (deep rose blooms) and 'William Baffin' (flowers the color of strawberry ice cream).

❦ 'Henry Kelsey', in particular, will send up fantastically vigorous long shoots when well-grown; when tied up, it will top an arch or trellis in a few seasons. Both its vigor and its sensational color make it the best red climbing rose available for cold areas.

❦ 'American Pillar', developed in the United States at the turn of the century, is also a popular hardy climber for Canadian gardens.

'American Pillar', a climbing rose, arches over the gate of this cottage in Chester, Nova Scotia.

ESTABLISHING CLIMBERS

❦ Since climbing roses (and roses that can be trained into climbers, such as the Explorers mentioned) produce long, vigorous shoots as they grow, they need to be tied to a support or structure. They also need to be trained; otherwise, shoots will arch in all directions with little regard for the shape or the confines of a trellis or arch. For maximum blooms, train branches to grow horizontally.

❦ When tying shoots, use material that will either break down with time or can be loosened to allow for future growth. Check ties annually and add new support as necessary.

❦ Once the plant is established, prune branches that grow outward, keeping those that are happy to grow near the support.

LATTICE SCREENS

Free-standing lattice screening has a multitude of uses in the garden.

❧ A simple square lattice screen (right) extends the line of a garden structure to create a garden room beyond it, and provides a backdrop for brilliant red and lemon-yellow climbing roses and a developing clematis.

❧ The inventive owner of this garden (below) used bold trellising painted a contrasting color to transform a garage wall into a striking year-round garden feature. The trellis is mounted to the wall on brackets for easy removal and maintenance. A lavabo and lion's mask add an air of antiquity to the setting, and echo the color and texture of the flagstone path. Lush hostas, succulent fall-blooming *Sedum spectabile* and the spiky foliage of ornamental grasses and daylilies provide a pleasing border.

TRELLIS TROMPE L'OEIL

Trellises can also be used to fool the eye and give a stucco wall year-round interest.

GARDEN ROOMS

Fences and trellises in a garden act like the walls, windows and doorways inside a house, leading the eye from one room to the next. A freestanding lattice screen (above) does double duty in this tranquil setting. Strongly architectural, it frames the difficult space between a wall of cedars and a lush yew hedge and successfully integrates the two garden areas, serving as the backdrop for one and the entrance to another. Diamond trelliswork with an arch of roses (below) frames a grass pathway into a garden room bordered with weathered planking.

The elegant trompe l'oeil (right) seems to recede into an alcove in the wall, providing an eye-catching foothold for brilliant red climbing roses.
(Above) Arching ferns, wild foamflower (*Tiarella cordifolia*) and native lady's-slipper orchids add to this delightful play of light, shadow and illusion.

STRIKING
STONE
WALLS

Sometimes mixing, rather than matching, materials makes a more dramatic point. The strong, clean lines of a lashed bamboo fence (top) crown a rough stone retaining wall. In keeping with the minimalist setting, clipped foliage and white flowers accent the muted tones of bamboo and stone.

In nature, plants often soften the bold presence of stone. Delicate *Corydalis lutea* embroiders the stones of a rugged wall (inset) with brilliant splashes of green and yellow. Thyme spills over a low wall (bottom) like a sheet of green water, smoothing the transition of the garden to a lower level.

A RUSTIC WATTLE FENCE

I f you've got strong hands and access to recently cut brushwood, consider building a bit of nostalgia — a nail-less wattle fence. Variously called wriggling, raddle, riddlin' or quiggly fences, these were once popular as windbreaks and livestock enclosures among farmers who either lacked nails or the money to buy them. In today's garden, they make attractive windbreaks for flower or vegetable beds, or supports for clematis or pole beans.

The fence consists of tightly spaced saplings woven through three horizontal wooden rails secured to upright posts. (In the photo above, horizontal wooden rails were used top and bottom only; a length of thick wire runs through the middle.)

CONSTRUCTION

1 Drive two posts about 2 feet (60 cm) into the ground, spaced 8 feet (2.4 m) apart. Cut notches in the posts to fit the rails like a mortise and tenon (you can bend the rules by nailing in the rails).

2 Use saplings no more than 1 inch (2.5 cm) in diameter and no more than 6 months old (older, thicker ones will not be supple and will be difficult to weave through the rails). Birch or willow is a good choice.

3 Strip away branches and foliage, then weave saplings vertically through the rails (and wire, if using) as snugly as possible. Make sure the bottom ends are at least a couple of inches above the ground to prevent rotting.

4 Trim the tops to an even height or leave them ragged. The bark eventually falls off the saplings and rails, leaving a weathered, rustic fence. It's easy to thread replacement saplings into place if some split or rot. To replace a rotted fence post, simply drive in a new one beside the old.

Through *the* Garden Gate

A contemporary gate as garden sculpture, a low gate to talk over, a tall gate to retreat behind — the style of a gate tells us a lot about a garden and its owner. It punctuates a fence or wall like an exclamation mark at the end of a sentence, exciting us to the possibility of what lies ahead.

E verything about this pretty wooden gate says "Welcome to my garden!" An ornamental grate set into the gate invites a peek into the vista beyond. Even the meandering path slows down a visitor's pace and encourages a closer look at the border plantings. A well-proportioned lattice border above solid boards softens the fence line while adding height and a measure of privacy.

Gates or fences need not always blend with a garden's color scheme or fade quietly into the background. Some make a strong statement of their own. A striking brick-red gate (right) adds its own note of color to a hot combination of pink foxgloves, orange California poppies and strawflowers.

Small details often add presence and personality to a garden. A simple arch over a gate of rounded pickets (above) frames the view into the garden more than the gate alone would do. Swags of lavender wisteria over the arch and the red leaves of a Japanese maple provide color accents in a background of early-summer foliage.

Add Rustic Charm
to Your Garden

*The appeal of
a twig gate is timeless
— and perfectly
in keeping with the
natural harmony of
any garden.*

A rustic twig gate, covered in a spring tiara of *Clematis montana*, offers a delightful welcome to a Vancouver garden. The design, by Ronae Theabeau of Delta, British Columbia, consists of two arches joined with side supports, creating a short tunnel; the doors are attached to the front arch. For each arch, you need a curved pole (B), which is nailed to two upright poles (A), each 3 to 4 inches (7.5 to 10 cm) in diameter. (Note: the dimensions and design of every gate will vary with available materials and the specific site. Use these instructions only as a guide.) To prevent rot, stand the bottom ends of the four upright poles in wood preservative overnight, or paint them with tar.

CONSTRUCTION

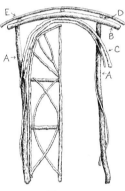

Front

*A-upright poles
B-curved pole for arch
C-support twigs
D-crosspieces
E-finishing twig*

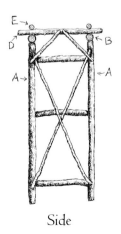

Side

1 Lay the first pair of upright poles (A) on a hard level surface. Insert temporary spreaders (scrap pieces of 1x2 will do) to ensure the opening is the same width top and bottom. Position the curved pole (B) at the top. Pre-drill all nail holes to prevent the wood from splitting. Nail in place with 6- or 7-inch (15 to 17.5 cm) galvanized spiral nails.

2 To strengthen the structure and keep the arches from leaning askew, carefully bend a couple of long twigs (C) and nail them in a curve under the top pole. Leave the twigs longer than necessary, and the nails protruding

slightly, in case adjustments are needed later. Repeat procedure on second arch.

3 Raise the two matching arches and connect them (about 18 inches/ 36 cm apart) with three crosspieces (D) nailed to the top of the curved poles (B). Nail three sturdy poles ladder fashion down each side (see Side view). To prevent the structure from tilting forward, nail two long twigs to the outside of the ladder, forming an X, and brace the side top corners with short twigs, forming triangles.

4 To finish the top, nail long twigs (E) over the crosspieces (D) on both front and back arches. Wind thin, supple willow twigs around the uprights for a decorative touch.

5 Set the arch on a level base, such as bricks with drainage holes or treated wood blocks. Add support stakes to hold the arch in place and use screws or lag bolts to attach them to the base.

6 Make the butterfly doors on flat ground. Make them 4 inches (10 cm) narrower than the inside width of the arch, to allow clearance on each side and some

space between the doors. Form each door from a straight central twig, an outer piece, curved to match the inside of the arch, and two or three crosspieces, each about 2 inches (5 cm) in diameter. Nail together as shown in the diagram and decorate the spaces with smaller twigs.

7 Attach each door to the ladder rungs of the side pieces using 1-inch (2.5 cm) eye screws set at right angles as hinges. The eyes are easily opened and closed with two pairs of pliers. Adjust the gap as needed to make the doors nearly touch in the center.

GARDEN STRUCTURES

*G*arden structures are irresistibly
romantic. If we close our eyes for a moment and imagine an idyllic garden scene,
it will probably include a structure of some kind — a summerhouse,
a vine-covered arbor or rose-laden arches over a pathway. These are special human
places within a natural setting. They provide shelter and privacy without isolating us
from the garden and offer a destination for even the briefest stroll.

Garden Romance.
You've Got *to* Get it Right.

Since a structure, more than any other feature, dictates the spirit of a garden, it is critical to understand how a gazebo, arbor or pergola will fit into the overall scheme before you erect it — and what site is most appropriate for it. Successful siting is the key to a well-integrated structure; otherwise, your garden will suffer with an irrelevant building, irrelevantly placed. To make sure you incorporate a structure naturally into your garden, consider the role it will play.

Is it *a* focal point?

As a focal point, a structure will attract or divert. In a large space, this allows you to establish directions; in a smaller space, it draws the eye inward and away from unattractive surroundings.

❧ A solid presence, such as a summerhouse or gazebo, can close a vista or strengthen the corner of a garden wall. It can also terminate a path or prompt further exploration through a wood.

❧ A lighter structure, such as a pergola or an arch, can define a pathway, divide a space or offer shaded passage from one area to another.

A structure close to the house, such as this one in downtown Toronto, should reflect the scale, mood and materials of the house. Farther away, the rustic or fanciful can take over.

Does it enhance *a* view?

Structures may be used to enhance or exploit a view — either as a lookout point over a wide vista or as a framing device.

❧ Overhead beams extending from the house, for example, create an outdoor room and frame the view from the house into the garden. A sculpture or specimen tree may also be framed by a simple, open structure occupying the middle ground.

What about scale *and* style?

❧ Close to the house, a structure should be large enough not to be dwarfed by the main building and should reflect the shapes, materials and colors of the house.

❧ A structure in a remote corner of the garden may be less formal — even rustic or eccentric — but it, too, must relate to its setting.

FRAMES *of* REFERENCE

It's useful to understand the architectural characteristics of gazebos, pergolas, arbors, arches and other structures before deciding which one suits your garden and lifestyle best. The goal is to create a pleasing, private outdoor space in which you can entertain, read quietly or simply sit and enjoy the view.

Arbors

An arbor is one of the simplest of garden structures — a wooden or metal form, covered in any manner of climbing plant, that provides a shady place to sit. Its Latin name indicates its intended function: to give the kind of shelter a tree might provide. A simple free-standing arbor, hand hewn from branches and left unadorned or encrusted with roses, adds focus to a garden and might invite passage to the spaces beyond.

Arches

Arches are very similar in shape to an arbor but do not provide shelter. Constructed of wood, metal, trelliswork or willow, they are most often used at the entrance to a garden or to frame the transition from one garden room to the next. Use them singly for an airy effect with a lacy climbing vine, or in a series to form a tunnel. A roof of green may be grown over a cross-weaving of wires or lattice — rampant vines such as Virginia creeper (*Parthenocissus quinquefolia*) and silver lace (*Polygonum aubertii*) make quick work of providing shade.

An ornate wooden gazebo, half-hidden under a tumble of flowers.

Bowers

Like an arbor, a bower also provides a cool, shady place to sit. Unlike an arbor, however, a bower depends primarily on natural elements, such as the boughs of trees trained to twine together, for its shape and structure. A sub-structure of wood or wire may be necessary to train and support the boughs.

Gazebos

Nothing captures the romance of a garden better than these fanciful summerhouses. Situated to command a view of the garden or the vista below, they provide a focal point and offer a peaceful retreat for entertaining or relaxing. Contemporary gazebos can imitate the ornate wrought-iron structures of the Victorian era or echo the clean lines of modern architecture.

Pergolas

A pergola is a structure that either links one part of the garden with another or simply provides a shaded walkway. Constructed of solid uprights and simple, strong beams, a pergola should be wide enough to allow two people to walk side by side. A covering of fast-growing vines provides additional shade and privacy.

Variations *on an* Arch

Positioned strategically at the end of a seaside garden in Chester, Nova Scotia, the simple yet striking white archway (above) frames a lovely view in either direction — from the bay, the charming Cape Cod-style house and garden and, from the porch, the bright blue waters of Mahone Bay. Colorful borders of phlox, shasta daisies, delphiniums, sweet William, campanula, pansies, strawflowers, poppies and asters add presence and appeal to both the pathway and its crowning arch.

A well-designed arch celebrates the spirit of the garden and the imagination of its owner.

A graceful willow arch entwined with clematis (right) marks the way into a delightful English country garden. Old-fashioned flowers — pink larkspur, blue *Campanula carpatica*, rose foxglove and columbine — brighten the meandering flagstone pathway that leads to the front door. A cedar picket fence, weathered to a soft grey, holds back generous plantings of yellow loosestrife (*Lysimachia punctata*) and deep blue delphinium.

A rose-laden arch (left) plays another role in this Vancouver garden. The owner constructed it to embellish a simple wooden boundary fence and gate and to frame the "borrowed" vista of a golf green beyond. Built simply and inexpensively of ladder-like wood strips wrapped in chicken wire, the arch is clothed in ivy all year long. From spring to late fall, clematis and climbing roses also bloom in succession. Here, 'Complicata' rose and 'Blue Ravine' clematis add color and lush foliage. Pacific Giant delphiniums and 'Iceberg' roses in pots flank the gate and lead the eye toward a row of distant Lombardy poplars.

A Passage *through* Pergolas

From the rustic to the romantic, pergolas offer a sheltered passageway from one garden space to another. Gertrude Jekyll, who set down the design rules for the 20th-century pergola, favored the following plants to grow over it: grapevine, Dutchman's-pipe (*Aristolochia durior*), Virginia creeper, wisteria, species clematis, trumpet vine (*Campsis radicans*), honeysuckle (*Lonicera* spp.), ivy (*Hedera* spp.) and roses. These can be used alone or in discreet combinations.

What better pergola (above) to lead us through the magical gardens of Merlin's Hollow in Aurora, Ontario, than one of gothic proportions. Already, pale rose clematis begins its quest to disguise the wooden frame of this whimsical structure. A densely planted border garden on either side strengthens the purpose and direction of the passageway and hints at the offerings of the garden room beyond.

A grapevine-clad pergola (right) dominates the back garden of a house situated in one of Toronto's many downtown neighborhoods. Practical and pretty at the same time, this Mediterranean-style structure frames the gravel pathway that leads to the back lane.

A s weathered as the split-rail fence bordering the country property, a simple wooden pergola (above) constructed in a grid pattern draws eyes and feet from one garden room to another. An unadorned wooden bench allows quiet enjoyment of the bed of early-summer blooms — peonies, orange lilies, white and pink foxgloves and campanulas.

PRUNING CLEMATIS

Canada's most popular flowering vine is undoubtedly the clematis, and for good reason. It provides a spectacular burst of brilliant flowers and offers a wonderful choice of form, shape and color: blooms that are pitcher-shape, bell-shape or flat, in shades of red, pink, yellow, purple or white; one color or bi-color; single or double. And it's hardy in most parts of the country, from Zones 3 to 8, depending on the hybrid or species. With a little care and proper selection of the species and cultivar that suit your site best, clematis will thrive and bloom in your garden for many years to come.

❧ The most important thing to know about the clematis you select is its flowering season — early or late spring, early or late summer, or fall. Its blooming time determines when the vine should be pruned.

❧ Proper pruning maximizes flower production. For the first two years, don't be concerned about blooms — prune for a multiplicity of stems to bear a multiplicity of flowers in the long term.

❧ Regardless of the type, prune all newly planted clematis to two sets of leaves or buds (about 6 inches/15 cm from the ground). Subsequent yearly pruning is dictated by the season of bloom.

❧ Vines that bloom in early spring flower on growth produced the previous year (old wood) which hardened off before the frost. In late winter, at the start of the plant's second season, prune all stems back to

Clematis 'Ville de Lyon'

a leaf bud about 36 inches (90 cm) above the ground. From the third season on, remove only dead or weak stems.

Examples: *C. montana,* the hardier *C. alpina* and hybrids, 'Duchess of Edinburgh' (fragrant double white), 'Miss Bateman' (white) and 'Nelly Moser' (pink stripe).

❧ Clematis that bloom in late spring or early summer produce flowers on new wood formed that year. Right after the second season's flowering, cut back all stems to a strong pair of buds at a height of 36 inches (90 cm). In the third and subsequent years, tip-prune all stems back to a set of leaves.

Examples: 'The President' (purple), 'Henryi' (white) and 'Mrs. Cholmondeley' (light blue).

❧ Late-flowering clematis also bear on the current year's growth. By next spring, all of this year's growth will have died off, so prune to ground level at the start of each season.

Examples: 'Comtesse de Bouchaud' (pink), 'Gipsy Queen' (violet), *C.* X *jackmanii* (purple), 'Ville de Lyon' (red) and the native *C. virginiana* (white).

Artful Arbors

The arbor perfectly combines the hard planes of architecture with the softer lines of nature.

Although arbors traditionally provide shelter or privacy, the word "arbor" may also be applied to a single-beam structure such as the one in the classical garden (above). The owner has used this style of arbor with arches to divide the garden into a series of inviting rooms with different themes.

An arbor is also an ideal way to hide the accoutrements of modern life, such as hydro meters, air-conditioning units and heat pumps. The post-and-beam arbor (right), designed with a Japanese flavor, artfully conceals an air-conditioning unit behind a screen of cedar slats while inviting visitors to the inner sanctum of the garden beyond. A hops vine on the right and climbing euonymus on the left soften the geometric lines of the cedar and contribute their own form of concealment.

CHAPTER THREE

FRONT YARDS

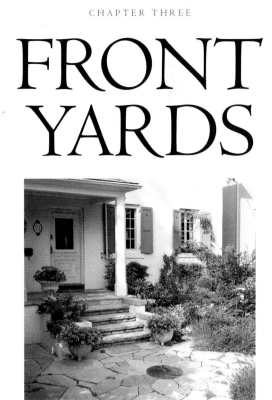

*T*he entrance
from the street to your house is
like a handshake or a smile — it's the
first impression visitors have
of the place where you live. And like
the human greeting, it reveals
a hint of your personality: homey and
welcoming, sophisticated but inviting,
or classically reserved.

Like a breath of fresh country air in the middle of a city street,
there's no mistaking the message this delightful front garden
(right) extends to friends and passersby alike.

Best Front Forward

A welcoming front yard depends on more than just imaginative plantings.

Front yards are a combination of charm and function. They should look great and work well at the same time. Successful front-yard design depends on a number of important elements — the way you use the whole space to lead visitors pleasantly and efficiently to the front door, the plants you choose to enhance the house and the broader streetscape, the materials you use for the pathway and how they are detailed, even the front door itself.

Paths

Front paths should welcome visitors, drawing them forward into your private space.

❧ Make the pathway generous enough to allow two people to walk side by side. If you can, widen the path at the front door to create a pleasant space for welcoming and leave-taking.

❧ Plot the obvious route from street to front door. Curves or jogs in a front path can be annoying unless they make practical sense and are reinforced by the general design of the garden.

❧ Be creative with the materials you choose. Consider the pattern in which the paving is laid, then add borders, raised edges or planting niches. Just remember that you will need to clear the path in snowy, icy weather!

❧ Achieve intimacy and style instantly with an archway over the path. Place garden sculpture as a focal point, or tuck it in among plantings as a surprise along the way.

Plantings

Since an entrance garden is a garden of passage, plantings should suit the style of the house and look good in all seasons.

❧ Look for plants with interesting form and foliage, harmonious colors and a variety of sizes and textures.

❧ For a smart, simple look and low maintenance, use a single specimen tree — Japanese maple, magnolia or birch — underplanted with an evergreen ground cover such as periwinkle or ivy.

❧ Transform a rough slope into a rock garden with bold ornamental grasses, creeping evergreens and bursts of perennial color.

❧ Mass pots and planters of bright annuals that change with the seasons, from spring pansies to summer impatiens and fall chrysanthemums.

Courtyards

A courtyard entry allows city dwellers to make full use of their limited garden space.

❧ For total seclusion, enclose the front yard with a tall hedge, fence or wall. Make sure the new structure is in keeping with the architecture of the house.

❧ Keep the plantings simple. Use walls and fences as vertical planting spaces for vines, espaliers or hanging planters.

❧ Heighten the feeling of intimacy with an attractive garden bench and the sound of water in a small fountain.

Doorways

The doorway itself is important. It should be dramatic because it is the symbolic point of transition from public to private space.

❧ Flank the doorway with matching topiary or richly planted urns for a formal look. For a country feel, place a rose- or vine-covered arch over the door.

❧ Paint the door a bold color — brick red, forest green or shiny black — and add a decorative doorknob, mailbox and door-knocker.

❧ Make sure the entryway is well lit. Good lighting adds charm in the summer, extends a warm welcome in the winter and makes your entry safe.

A COUNTRY-STYLE FRONT GARDEN

Planted with a reckless gaiety that is the hallmark of English cottage gardens, this horticultural feast for the eyes (featured on previous page and in detail below) bursts with color from early spring until the last crisp days of fall.

❦ In spring, there are bulbs — narcissus, tulips, muscari and crocus.

❦ In early summer, a tree peony opens its luscious big blossoms by the front steps, and yellow globeflowers (*Trollius* spp.) grace the beds.

❦ Midsummer brings tall coral phlox, pink musk mallow (*Malva moschata*), lilies of all types, hydrangea, yarrow (*Achillea* X 'Moonshine'), roses ('Iceberg' and 'Peace'), gooseneck loosestrife (*Lysimachia clethroides*), delphiniums and rose campion (*Lychnis coronaria*).

❦ September features the pie-size blooms of a hardy hibiscus (*H. moscheutos* 'Southern Belle').

❦ Annuals are used extensively in the garden to give a long season of color. Impatiens, lobelia and sweet alyssum tumble onto the path, while tall spider flower (*Cleome spinosa*) and cosmos planted among the perennials add ongoing bursts of color.

❦ The picket fence is swagged with bright blue morning glories for late-summer color and with lovely lavender clematis 'Ramona'.

❦ Wreathed with 'Blaze Improved', a classic and dependable climbing rose, the window also supports a long wooden planter overflowing with yellow tuberous begonias, purple pansies and dainty lobelia.

❦ In keeping with the cottage theme, a picket fence surrounds the property. From the front gate, a meandering path of crushed brick leads to the front steps, bordered with brightly planted terra-cotta pots. An old-fashioned gingerbread-trimmed wooden screen door completes the charming country welcome.

Make a Splash *with* Color

A change of paint on walls, shutters, verandahs and fences is one of the easiest ways to add front-yard interest to your home.

From boring beige to beautiful! The owners of this once-ordinary house in St. Catharines, Ontario, gave it a new lease on life by painting it a vibrant blue, with rose shutters that match their favorite fibrous begonias. The rosy tones also pick up the color of the reclaimed brick used as trim on the house. The color scheme also pulls together the foundation plantings — mugho pine, barberry and golden mock orange. The inspirational begonias, in terra-cotta pots set into holes in a blue-painted shelf, brighten the view from the kitchen window, at right.

Bright and cheerful as a summer's day, these delightful cottage-style homes on Toronto's Ward's Island make exuberant use of color, with very pleasing results.

❧ Splashed against a white picket fence, yellow daylilies, rose campion and creeping bellflower shine against the electric blue walls of the cottage (above), like wildflowers under a brilliant summer sky.

❧ The mustard shutters and cool green walls of the house (below) provide a rich background for the graceful ferns that border the walls, and for the blue irises, buttercups, wild phlox, mimulus and white impatiens that bloom in front.

VARIATIONS IN STONE

Everything about this entrance (inset) exudes a

country charm, even though there isn't a blade of grass in sight. The striking floral inset, designed from slate-grey and sand-color flagstones, provides the focal point for the property. Slate-grey shutters and roof tiles against pale-yellow stucco walls echo the muted warmth of the flagstone courtyard and steps. Stone planters brimming with pink blooms add a bright accent.

These eye-catching front yards are an attractive alternative to high-maintenance front lawns.

Imposing stone slabs, implanted with purple pansies and pink geraniums, form the steps and retaining wall of a well-designed front-yard garden (above). The presence of a towering weeping cypress left of the steps provides the big hit of green that an expanse of lawn normally would. A fast-growing vine, spreading along the steps and up the house walls, softens the bold lines of the stone and unites house and front yard.

The front yards of these two houses reflect the elegance of the architecture and the style of the owners. Symmetrically placed ornate stone planters (above) grace the formal arched entrance to a stone house in Toronto's affluent Rosedale district. A simple herringbone brick path (left) leads to the front door of a Georgian-style limestone house in Burritts Rapids, Ontario. Black shutters and a fan arch over the front door echo the original architectural style of the period.

There isn't an easier front yard to maintain than this understated, rustic one (left) in downtown Toronto. From the weathered lashed-bamboo fences that border the garden to the crushed stone that provides texture and presence, each element contributes to the overall harmony of the setting. Lush plantings of fern and climbing euonymus by the verandah add a green note to the pleasing palette of earth tones.

A GARDEN
of GRASSES

These ornamental grasses are among the most striking and the easiest to incorporate into garden settings. Each can be used alone or in combination with other grasses.

Bulbous oat grass (*Arrhenatherum elatius bulbosum* 'Variegata') is the most popular of six tuberous oat grasses. It has green and white striped leaves, grows one to two feet (30 to 60 cm) tall and is recommended for massing in sun or partial shade. Small enough to be useful in a rock garden setting. Zone 4.

Feather reed grass (*Calamagrostis* X *acutiflora* 'Karl Foerster') starts the season in May as a two-foot (60 cm) clump of green stalks, and in June sprouts four-foot

Ornamental Grasses

As gardeners look for elegant architectural foliage and a natural appearance for their gardens, perennial grasses are making a comeback. Stalks and plumes sway in the slightest breeze, creating a garden in motion — a landscape that changes from minute to minute on the whim of the wind. Grasses can transform a dull, flat space into undulating waves of color and texture. Much of their appeal also lies in the autumn and winter interest they contribute to the garden.

Dwarf Fountain Grass   *Japanese Silver Grass*

(120 cm) stems with feathery pink tufts. The tufts turn light purple in July, gold in the fall and last most of the winter. Form is upright and the translucent tufts glow in the sun. Looks best in groups or drifts. Zone 4.

Blue lyme grass (*Elymus racemosus* 'Glaucus') has an irregular form about three feet (90 cm) tall and is ideal in small groups in the mid-border, or in masses in sunny areas. Its aggressive tendencies may need to be curtailed. Zone 4.

Manna grass (*Glyceria maxima* 'Variegata') has white to yellow two-inch (5 cm) variegated leaves. It is happiest in moist areas (near ponds, in bog gardens or along streams) and will prevent soil erosion along stream banks. Brightens dull areas. Zone 5.

Blue oat grass (*Helictotrichon sempervirens*) has two-

to three-foot (60 to 90 cm) blue-grey foliage lasting through the year. Beautiful in the middle of the border, harmonizing with blue perennials and accenting gold or yellow flowers. The tan flower sprays that appear in summer are carried three feet (90 cm) above the leaves. Prefers good drainage in a dry area. Zone 4.

Japanese silver grass (*Miscanthus sinensis* 'Gracillimus') grows four to six feet (120 to 180 cm) tall, with

arching white and green striped leaves. The plumes bloom reddish-pink, then turn beige in early October and last through the winter. They make good cut or dried flowers. Japanese silver grass is useful for damp areas, or as a screen or border. Zone 5.

Variegated silver grass (*Miscanthus sinensis* 'Variegatus') grows three to five feet (120 to 150 cm) tall and has yellow, white and green striped leaves, with colorful feathery plumes in late summer.

A perfect focal plant for the fall garden. Zone 5.

Porcupine grass (*Miscanthus sinensis* 'Strictus') grows eight feet (240 cm) tall, with horizontal yellow and green stripes in the leaves. The plant form is stiff and upright, with bronze to red plumes that change to silver as the seeds mature. Zone 5.

Zebra grass (*Miscanthus sinensis* 'Zebrinus') grows five to seven feet (150 to 210 cm) tall and is noted for its unique

alternating yellow and green bands on the leaves. The plumes, yellow in September, turn to tan in winter. Grows in moist soil. Zone 5.

Dwarf fountain grass (*Pennisetum alopecuroides* 'Hameln') has two-foot (60 cm) leaves, with taller silvery-rose flower plumes from July to October. It's a magnificent sight in the fall garden, and provides a wealth of plumes for dried flower arrangements. Zone 5.

CHAPTER FOUR

PATHS
&STEPS

*P*aths and the steps
that connect them are the ground
plan of a garden, the key elements
that define and unite its spaces.
They establish how we move
through a garden and how we
view the plantings inside, or the
vistas outside, our private domain.
At its best, this hard landscaping
takes on an almost sculptural
quality and sets the mood of the
whole garden.

An elegant yet simple flagstone path winds provocatively
through a garden, dividing the space into islands of bloom
and luring the visitor onward.

Down *the* Garden Path

A good garden path is esthetically pleasing, both in surface and in style.

Pathways are the invitations extended by our garden — they lead us into the garden and entice us to go on. Paths can be as casual as a meandering swath of green cutting through banks of brilliant wildflowers or an intricately patterned stone walkway that leads to a secluded wrought-iron bench. Whatever the reason for a path, here's how to make each small journey on it an enjoyable one.

Plotting a Path

Although the purpose of a path is to get from one place to another, the way in which you lay out the steps for that passage influences the overall look and appeal of your garden. Since a path becomes the backbone of a garden scheme, consider the style, shape and direction that works best in your own setting — then structure a path that will enhance your overall design.

❧ Emphasize or minimize a garden's length by striking a straight path that accentuates lines down or across the space.

❧ Use a path to divide the garden into a series of distinct areas or garden rooms. To add a sense of space or to intrigue, place the plants in each room so that they partially conceal the other areas from view.

❧ Slow the pace with a narrow, meandering, finely detailed path that allows time to pause over the garden's tiniest plant.

A SWATH *of* GRASS

Like a green runner spilling from room to room, a pathway of grass offers one of the simplest yet most sensuous invitations to the garden.

In a quiet country setting, a swath of mown grass (left) cuts decisively through woods overarched with weeping willows, maples, locust and bamboo.

Be Creative *with* Materials

The materials you use also play an important role in your overall design scheme. Select materials that complement the style of both the house and the surrounding property — paying particular attention to textures, patterns or colors that will enhance the look of the garden and create the mood you want.

❧ Lay stones with enough space between them to encourage invasion of creeping plants such as thyme, ajuga, golden Scotch moss (*Sagina subulata* 'Aurea') or prostrate veronica.

❧ Set stones in decorative patterns to create an ornamental pathway that complements both simple and formal planting schemes.

❧ Add texture — and instant antiquity — to paths of poured concrete by impressing the still-damp surface with large leaves such as water lilies or hostas. Once the concrete has dried, the foliage will disintegrate and leave behind a delicate print.

❧ Set large, random-shape slabs and smaller stones in fine gravel to make a pathway suited to a country setting.

❧ Plant low-growing herbs, such as thyme and creeping chamomile, here and there in a gravel path — they add a heavenly fragrance when walked on.

❧ For a natural look, cover a simple earth path with recycled tree trimmings or wood chips.

A broad sweep of grass (below) mimics the shape of the undulating flower beds and flows invitingly across the garden toward a strategically placed lawn chair — and a moment's pause to enjoy the view.

Marking the end of one garden room and the beginning of another, a manicured path (right) leads the visitor past dramatic beds of white and purple hydrangea and snow-in-summer to the stone terrace a few steps above.

GRAVEL PATHS

Gravel paths were used extensively in Victorian times and look wonderful beside borders of old roses, shasta daisies and delphiniums. They also work well in Oriental gardens.

❧ Before laying a gravel path, make sure the surface is level to prevent washouts in heavy rain. Place a geotextile fabric liner over the soil to keep weeds from sprouting and to allow drainage through the stones. Cover with a 2- to 3-inch (5 to 7.5 cm) layer of gravel.

❧ Edgings are needed to keep the gravel confined and to give the path a finished look. Attractive rope edgings, once popular in Victorian gardens, are enjoying a revival; they are available at a number of garden centers.

❧ (Above) The owner of this half-acre rural property in southern Ontario replaced a high-maintenance lawn with a number of small gardens — all linked by winding paths of gravel. Ground covers, such as the creeping thyme at left, soften the pathways and trail from one garden room to another, weaving the individual spaces together.

❧ (Inset) Tucked away in a quiet corner of a Japanese-inspired garden, this striking path underscores the owner's sensitivity to form and texture. Round concrete pavers, randomly placed within the gravel, beg a visitor's steps and encourage a slower pace past airy ferns and Siberian irises that grow at the base of a simple bamboo trellis.

GREEN VELVET

Like emerald-green puddles in the City of Oz, moss splashes through the striking stepping-stone path of natural and man-made stones (right). Note the intricate leaf and flower impressions set into the foremost slab (see how-to, p. 43). A broad sweep of rich, dark earth anchors both stones and moss.

FRAGRANT WALKWAYS

There's nothing more soothing to the spirit than a quiet walk over a thyme-covered path. Each gentle crush of footsteps releases a delightful fragrance — sweet or pungent, depending on the variety of thyme. These delicate paths suit lower-traffic areas best. A carpet of pink creeping thyme (top left) washes over a weathered flagstone path. Equally at home in a city setting, mats of Scotch moss and thyme (bottom left) soften the flagstone walkway that runs between the front and side entrances of a suburban home.

MAKE YOUR OWN HERB PATH

Creeping thymes are best suited for herb paths; they're low-growing and require little upkeep. Consider 'Doone Valley' lemon thyme, a gold-variegated scented variety; wild thyme, low and wonderfully scented; caraway thyme, also scented; and/or unscented woolly thyme, with grey leaves and tiny pink flowers.

HERE'S WHAT TO DO

1 Outline the area, including a border of soil on either side of the path for planting the herbs.

2 Dig out soil, the width of the path, to a depth of 4 inches (10 cm). An edging of wood is advisable to keep the path neat and to prevent soil from falling onto the path.

3 Spread 2 inches (5 cm) of sharp sand over the base; level and dampen. Lay the bricks on top of the sand in the desired pattern, leaving a 1/4-inch (5 mm) gap between them. Using a mallet, settle the bricks into the sand.

4 Plant small herbs about a hand-span apart; within a short space of time, they will grow into each other, softening the edges of the path.

THE BEAUTY OF BRICK

Brick has been used in gardens around the world for many hundreds of years to make pathways, patios, walls, lawn edgings and more. It comes in a wide range of colors, is durable and colorfast, and won't decay if it's properly installed and maintained.

Brick paths have warmth, a pleasing patina — and long life, if you use the proper brick. Make sure you choose hard, impervious brick that has been fired completely. For a contemporary look, consider tan or grey brick; for an informal look, curve the path or allow clumps of thrift (*Armeria*) or rock cress (*Arabis*) to grow in soft mounds over the edges.

❧ An intricate basketweave pattern (top), enhanced by edgings of soft green moss, transforms a simple brick walkway into an elegant architectural tapestry.

❧ Herbs and lamb's-ears spilling over the edge of a brick parquet path (left) lend it a casual air, as does its gentle curve.

❧ A tightly laid path of soft grey brick (opposite) opens up into an intimate courtyard — the perfect spot for a table and some comfy twig chairs. Tall ornamental grasses and a screen of evergreens ensure privacy and provide a pleasing contrast to the brick and twig.

CONVERSATION PIECES

Unusual objects can also be integrated into a garden setting to provoke interest or add an air of antiquity. Old millstones enliven the design of this loosely laid flagstone path. Their color and circular shape echo the shape and texture of the stones — for a harmonious blending of unlike objects into a pleasing whole.

Even a single step makes the slightest change in level more exciting, while a flight of steps can be spectacular.

Easy Steps *to a* Great Garden

Perfect paths deserve perfect steps, and steps can do wonderful things for your garden. They are interesting to look at and to use, they create a sense of expectation and their strong lines contrast with the softness of growing things. Steps also draw our eyes downward, giving us the opportunity to discover — and enjoy — the fine details of the garden as we move from one level to another.

Step Styles

When considering even a single step, remember to choose materials that complement the garden path and suit the mood of the surroundings.

❧ For simple steps in an informal setting, wooden treads and stone slabs are effective partners. Using two materials eases the transition from house to garden, the move from constructed to natural.

❧ Cross sections of a fallen tree trunk, treated with preservative, make marvelous steps in a woodland setting. Arrange them to follow the contour of the slope and generously plant around them with creeping ground covers, which are in keeping with the natural style of the garden.

❧ The width of a step is also important in the overall design. Steep, narrow steps suggest a brisk climb, while shallow, wide ones inspire a slower pace.

A ROCK GARDEN WITH A DIFFERENCE

Like the ever-widening ripples left by a stone dropped into water, circles of shallow steps surround a delightful flower-encrusted flagstone patio in St. Andrew's-by-the-Sea, New Brunswick. Different shades of stone were used deliberately, both to create visual interest and to complement the blue color of the charming shingled house.

THE CRUNCH *of* GRAVEL

Wide gravel steps banded by wooden risers (below) are one of the easiest and most economical of garden staircases to construct. They are particularly suited to larger properties — such as this recent garden renovation in Durham, Ontario. The steps have been broken up with generous landings that provide space for a strategically placed wrought-iron bench. The width of the steps also encourages a relaxed journey through the garden, with time to enjoy the summer show of bright orange lilies, yellow and dusky-red daylilies and pale pink astilbe.

STEPS *of* STONE

Although the medium — stone — is the same for the three step designs above and at left, the message is creatively different in each case.

❧ Bulblet ferns and soft green moss, tucked into the risers, transform imposing stone pavers (left) into a gently ascending natural staircase. The generous size of the stone works with the shallow rise of each step to encourage a slow, leisurely ascent.

❧ A high, solid flight of mortared stone steps (top) allows easy passage from the lower level of a Vancouver garden to the top of the densely planted slope. Pots of blooms add a splash of color.

❧ Creeping phlox spills over flagstone steps (above) that lead to a front door, softening and redefining the straight lines of the stone.

CHAPTER FIVE

USING PLANTS *for* EFFECT

❦

*P*lants in a garden are like
the actors on a stage. Some, like extravagant pink peonies, are the showy
flowers of the production. Others, like a stretch of silver lamb's-ears or lush
green hostas, provide the supporting background that enhances or
separates dramatic bursts of color. Even unobtrusive vines add an everchanging
curtain of foliage. No matter how large or small, the role of each plant
is integral to the success of the overall garden scheme. Here's how to use
plants to best effect in your own garden.

Foliage – A Garden Essential

*Foliage relies
primarily on its
leaves, rather than on
blooms, to make an
impact in the garden.*

Foliage is an important architectural element in a garden, the supporting framework upon which the rest of the design is shaped. Unlike flowers, which rely primarily on bursts of color to make an impression, foliage contributes long-lasting texture and lushness, and provides a dramatic backdrop for other plants. It also acts as a unifying element, weaving together the many separate spaces of a garden into a harmonious whole.

From a leafy camouflage of Virginia creeper that disguises an unsightly shed to a delicate sweep of ferns that enlivens a shady corner, you'll find that foliage offers an attractive solution to many of the design dilemmas in your garden.

Leaves are a Many-Splendored Thing

Whether you're redesigning a tiny corner of your garden or starting from scratch with a much grander plan, don't overlook the decorative potential of leafy plants.

❧ Hostas, ferns and ground covers contribute a sensuous, almost tactile, quality to the garden and come in a dazzling range of verdant colors — from the heavily textured blue-grey foliage of *Hosta sieboldiana* 'Elegans' to the glossy evergreen leaves and dainty flowers of periwinkle (*Vinca minor*).

❧ Under the protective shelter of trees, shrubs, garden walls or the soffit of a house, shade-loving leafy plants provide movement, texture and a constantly changing pattern of light and shadow.

❧ Our pick of the most popular leafy plants begins on the next page. All are readily available across the country, thrive with little care and make a striking addition to any garden. Best of all, they're guaranteed to get you started on your own love affair with the leaf.

FERNS

Ferns, like many other woodland plants, look best in a setting that replicates their natural environment. In other words, plant them to look as though they've always been there. The feathery, light-green fronds invite the gentle play of breezes and add beautiful grace notes to any garden. Varying in height from a few inches to a few feet, ferns thrive in cool, shaded areas and look equally impressive on their own or in a casual grouping of rocks or against half-rotted stumps or logs. Ferns are also easy to move from one spot to another in a garden; the best time to do this is in the spring, before the fiddleheads have unfurled into full leaf.

This delightful pairing of ferns with a fanciful garden ornament (an exuberant fish wrought in stone) reminds us that the best approach to gardening is always a lighthearted one.

HOSTAS

Hostas come in a remarkable range of colors, shapes, textures and sizes, and make a dramatic statement anywhere in the garden. Although they are a member of the lily family and produce delicate pastel flowers in mid- or late summer, hostas are relied on primarily for the striking beauty of their leaves.

❧ Their foliage varies from the deepest greens and greeny-blues to softly washed greens and yellows; the variegated forms add edgings of white, cream, gold or green.

❧ Leaves may be cupped, lance-shape or heart-shape, while leaf edges can be wavy or even slightly ridged. In texture, the foliage may be smooth, ribbed, ruffled or puckered, and leaf surfaces range from glossy to matte to almost frosted.

❧ Depending on where you place hostas and the size you choose, they can neatly mask the dying foliage of spring bulbs, fill in around leggy plants or provide a tall backdrop for other elements within the garden.

❧ Plant several different hostas together and let their contrasting shapes and colors add a bold accent to the garden. Or, mass a single species around a tree or at the edge of a pathway for dramatic effect.

The variegated foliage of Hosta sieboldiana *'Frances Williams' (top) lightens a planting of the 'Elegans' cultivar. The contrasting textures, colors and leaf shapes of these two hostas create a dramatic sweep of lushness within a verdant woodland setting.* Hosta lancifolia *in full summer bloom (above) provides a bold accent for an edging of ribbon grass.*

THESE HOSTAS ARE HOT!

❧ *Hosta plantaginea* 'Grandiflora'. The handsome bright green, heart-shape leaves reach 2 feet (60 cm). Its late-summer flowers are extremely large, white and fragrant. Does well in woodland settings as well as sunnier sites.

❧ *Hosta sieboldiana* 'Elegans'. A massive plant well over 2 feet (60 cm) tall, with large, broad leaves up to a foot (30 cm) wide. Bluish-grey leaves are puckered and crinkled; white to pale-lilac flowers in July add to its elegance. Use as an accent in clumps or alone in planters around a courtyard or patio.

❧ *Hosta sieboldiana* 'Frances Williams'. Bluish-grey leaves are edged with gold. A single plant can reach 3 feet (90 cm), with a 4-foot (120 cm) spread. It makes a strong statement in the shade.

❧ *Hosta lancifolia*. This species has narrow, waxy-green leaves that overlap each other to make a distinct, symmetrical mound. Leaves are up to 6 inches (15 cm) long and 2 inches (5 cm) wide. Plants grow 18 inches (45 cm) tall. Lavender flowers appear in late summer. Good as a ground cover or for edging.

❧ *Hosta venusta*. Slightly wavy dark-green leaves are 2 to 3 inches (5 to 8 cm) long; violet flowers appear in early summer. Since the plant's overall height is only about 5 inches (13 cm), it should be planted in a rockery or raised bed where it can be appreciated.

GROUND COVERS

If you're tired of looking after a high-maintenance lawn or just need to fill a hole in the garden where nothing else will grow, an attractive ground cover may be the answer.

❦ Ground covers creep into gardens, sometimes uninvited; as they spread, they carpet the surrounding landscape as nature would, filling out spaces and incorporating other plants into their growth pattern for pleasing effect.

❦ They provide a natural protection for the soil, holding in moisture and keeping weeds at bay; they also help prevent soil erosion on slopes. Since most common ground covers, such as English ivy, sweet woodruff or ajuga, thrive with very little sun and water, they are ideal in gardens where low maintenance or natural gardening are considerations.

❧ Their shallow roots and high tolerance for shade also make them well suited for planting in the shadow of mature trees where little else survives.

❧ Although ground covers can be invasive, once you know how to put their free-roaming spirit to constructive use in your garden, you'll be delighted with the quick results.

❧ For pathways or among flagstones, choose low-to-the-ground carpeters that form tight mats and invite footsteps. Low-growing plants like ajuga spread quickly into a leafy carpet or edging, while taller plants with a mounding habit (hardy geraniums are an example) have more texture and presence.

❧ In sunnier spots, a tapestry effect of different varieties of thyme is a fragrant solution.

EFFORTLESS GROUND COVERS

Creeping Jenny (*Lysimachia nummularia*)
❧ Also called moneywort, this very low ground cover grows wild from Newfoundland to the West Coast and is easily recognized by its shiny, coin-like leaves and tiny star-like yellow flowers that light up the ground in early summer. Hardy and aggressively invasive, creeping Jenny is well suited to edging pathways or tumbling over terraced slopes.

Bugleweed (*Ajuga*)
❧ In late spring, the flower spires of ajuga rise above dense rosettes of leaves, heralding summer's arrival with a swath of rich blue or pink. After a few weeks, the spikes die down, leaving a carpet of glossy, dark green or variegated leaves — hence the common name, carpet bugle. Ajuga, a member of the mint family, also works well tucked into the spaces of a flagstone path, or along stone walls and the risers of stone steps. The leaves of this quick-spreading plant come in a number of color variations, including dramatic shades of red and purple.

Pachysandra
❧ Also known as Japanese spurge, this versatile, drought-tolerant evergreen grows about 10 inches (25 cm) tall and is ideal for covering large areas, especially under trees. The broad, glossy green leaves, with serrated edges, contribute lush texture to the garden.

Periwinkle (*Vinca minor*)
❧ This is one of the prettiest and most popular of the low-lying ground covers, with glossy evergreen leaves and dainty white, blue or purple flowers that bloom in early spring. Plant in dappled or medium shade and be sure to keep soil fairly moist.

Lily-of-the-Valley (*Convallaria majalis*)
❧ Lush, shiny green leaves and delicately perfumed bell-shaped flowers in spring make this a delightful old-fashioned addition to any garden. Later in summer, the dark green foliage fills in around taller plants and provides a cooling contrast.

Baltic or English Ivy (*Hedera helix*)
❧ This vine-like evergreen ground cover can be planted in either sun or shade. If it's in a site it likes, it may spread tenaciously.

English Ivy with Hosta

The Lushness *of* Vines

QUICK COVER-UPS

I f it's time to take control of an eyesore or fill a gap in the greenery, be bold — call on a vigorous annual vine. With its lush foliage and blooms, it will provide your garden with almost instant gratification.

❧ Because annual vines reach maturity in one season, they're great for hiding an eyesore until a permanent planting is established, or a trellis or screen can be installed.

❧ They're also a big plus if you're gardening on rented property or are planning to move soon and don't want to invest in perennial vines. Most can be started from seed, and remain inexpensive even if you buy new seed year after year.

❧ Annual vines can also help in garden planning by standing in for a perennial vine while you decide whether you've chosen the best spot for a permanent climber.

❧ While morning glory and scarlet runner beans are the annual vines most commonly grown in Canada, there are many other dramatic and colorful varieties from exotic places like New Zealand or California that thrive equally well in our hot summers and last right up to the first frost.

Bottle Gourd (*Lageneria siceraria*)

This is not a plant for the timorous, or for the gardener who likes to be in control; on the other hand, it will easily disguise your neighbor's garage by early August.

❧ The seeds are large and can either be started indoors in peat pots or planted directly outside once the weather is

Bottle Gourd

warm enough. Two plants easily cover an area about 16 feet by 8 feet (5 by 2.5 m).

❧ Gourds need a strong support, such as a sturdy wooden trellis; they're both too heavy and too fragile to be grown with string as a support. You may need to tie stems to the crosspieces.

❧ Because the bottle gourd is a tropical plant, it doesn't make real progress until the weather and soil warm up. Once it starts to grow, though, it does so at breakneck speed — putting on about a foot a day — and demands only heat and water.

❧ The plant is a member of the squash and cucumber family. The male flowers are white and contrast well with the plant's large and fleshy dark green leaves; the female flowers resemble miniature green gourds. Flowers open early in the morning or just before sunset, and close in full sun.

Cup-and-Saucer Vine (*Cobaea scandens*)

In many ways, this vine is the opposite of the bottle gourd.

❧ It's slower to mature, reaching 8 feet (2.5 m) in early August, and is at its best in late August or September.

❧ The blooms open in full daylight and the plant, although vigorous, grows in a disciplined, orderly manner, never sending out shoots in all directions like the bottle gourd.

❧ Its delicate white or mauve-pink flowers form the cup, which opens from the green saucer of the calyx. Each pale green leaf clings closely to the stem but moves in the wind; all the leaves are identical and exactly the same distance from the support.

❧ To give seeds a head start, plant them in peat pots a few weeks before the last frost. The vines need a sturdy support such as a wood trellis, but trendrils will cling to poles.

Hyacinth Bean (*Dolichos lablab*)

This sturdy, upright vine looks best on a low fence — the flowers and pods stand up in clusters and show much better than on a tall support.

❧ Although the leaves and flowers are shaped like the scarlet runner bean and its other edible bean cousins, the colors of the blooms and stems are different — flowers are purple-pink or white, and the stems and flower buds a deep, red-purple. The purple-pink variety is especially attractive, with short, lustrous burgundy pods that stay on the vine for the whole season.

❧ Start seeds indoors in peat pots a few weeks before the last frost. The first flowers appear when the plants are 12 to 15 inches (30 to 40 cm) tall; blooms continue until the first frost.

Cup-and-Saucer Vine

Wild Cucumber (*Echinocystis lobata*)

For a touch of the unusual, grow wild cucumber. Its spiny seed pods appear in early August and hang down like ornaments on a Christmas tree. The foliage resembles pale-green miniature grape leaves.

❧ Also called wild balsam apple, this prolific vine doesn't start to grow until the days warm up. In one summer, it can almost cover an area 12 feet by 3 feet (3.5 m by 90 cm) but maintains a delicate look.

❧ The seed pods — small spiny balls, about the size of a plum and soft to the touch — last until the first severe frost. Toward the end of the season, the bottom of each pod opens and you can see the large seeds tucked inside two spongy compartments. If you don't remove them, the plant will self-seed profusely.

❧ Small white flowers, massed together and standing above the foliage, produce a frothy effect similar to silver lace vine (*Polygonum aubertii*).

❧ Since it's often difficult to buy seed, look for plants in the wild, such as along railroad tracks, and harvest a few pods. Plants grow easily from seed sown outdoors after danger of frost has passed.

Wild Cucumber

PERENNIAL FAVORITES

Like their annual cousins, perennial vines also play a number of important supporting roles in the garden. They may take longer to cover a trellis or fence, but grow vigorously once established. Use them to make the most of vertical growing space in small areas, to create a spectacular display of flowers or simply to provide a welcome canopy of shade. The most popular of the perennial vines are Virginia creeper, clematis, wisteria, English ivy, climbing hydrangea and honeysuckle.

Vines can help create different degrees of shade and privacy, depending on how densely the leaves grow and how high and overarching the garden structure is.

The lush appeal of Virginia creeper (Parthenocissus quinquefolia) *is not limited to one season. It tumbles over a wooden fence (right) in glorious autumn splendor.*

THE APPEAL *of* CLIMBING HYDRANGEA

Climbing hydrangea (*Hydrangea anomala petiolaris*) makes an attractive addition to any garden.

🌺 Softly scented creamy-white flowers cover this vigorous deciduous climber in June and give it a dainty look — even though its lustrous heart-shape leaves form a dense cover.

🌺 Climbing hydrangea's growth pattern is on more than one plane; a few branches arch gracefully away from their support, creating a two-dimensional tiered effect that casts interesting shadows on the ground below.

🌺 The vine's full, rich texture makes it a good candidate to romp over stumps or rock piles or scramble along the base of a large terrace as a lush ground cover. Or use its shiny leaves as a contrasting backdrop in a mixed border.

🌺 The tiny aerial rootlets of climbing hydrangea (like those of English ivy) cluster along the stems and cling to flat surfaces; a brick wall or unfinished wood fence gives the best support. A young vine may need to be tied to its support until it is accustomed to the site.

🌺 Buy a container-grown specimen (hydrangea resents having its roots disturbed), and don't expect much growth the first few years. Plant in rich, moist soil and prune in early spring to keep it under control, if necessary. This flowering vine is one of the few that grows well even on a north-facing wall.

🌺 Leaves turn a pale gold in autumn, and the handsome cinnamon-brown bark of mature branches is shaggy and papery — a textural highlight in the winter garden. Climbing hydrangea is hardy to Zone 5. Mature vines may eventually reach 70 feet (21 m).

The Fine Art *of* Espalier

If your garden is too small for bushy shrubs or fruit trees, fanciful espalier might be the answer.

The art of training ornamental shrubs or dwarf trees to grow in flat patterns, usually against a wall or fence, dates back to Roman times and was widely used in medieval Europe. This pruning technique tailors spreading trees into eye-catching two-dimensional wall features.

❧ Espalier can add to the appearance of any garden, small or large, and is especially lovely against a stark modern wall. Since all branches are exposed to direct sunlight and the vigor of the main branches is controlled with pruning, espaliered trees produce large, early yields of high-quality fruit.

Espaliered trees or shrubs can be used in the garden in a number of dramatic ways. Like a striking natural sculpture, a horizontally espaliered dwarf pear (above) decorates and softens the bare white siding of an otherwise unadorned house.

❦ The short, compact shapes — rarely taller than 6 or 7 feet (180 to 210 cm) when fully mature — are easy to maintain. Many varieties can be grown in areas colder than their normal climatic zone if they're planted against a sun-reflecting, south-facing wall or fence.

❦ You could also try freestanding espalier. On its own support of posts and wires, it doubles as a hedge or fence to delineate property boundaries or separate a large garden into small areas. It's also a useful, attractive and space-saving edging around laneways, walkways, pools, decks and patios.

What trees or shrubs are suitable?

Today's most popular choices for espalier are dwarf trees, usually apple or pear, which grow fruit on permanent fruiting spurs. Once trained to the desired shape, they don't produce a lot of succulent growth, and can be kept neat with a little regular summer pruning.

❦ Stone fruits — peaches, plums, cherries, apricots and nectarines — bear fruit on short-lived spurs and produce a great deal of vegetative growth. They are harder to keep under control and are a poor choice for tidy-looking espalier in a small space.

❦ Choose shrubs or trees that produce flowers or fruit on old wood and tolerate severe pruning and training. A shrub that flowers from the base, such as the snowball hydrangea or potentilla, won't work. In addition to pear and apple, try cotoneaster, some hollies, crab apple, firethorn (*Pyracantha*), currant (*Ribes*), viburnum, grape (*Vitis*) or wisteria.

Where do I start?

Establishing espalier isn't difficult, but it does require time and patience.

❦ First, make sure you have a suitable location; it should get a minimum of six hours of sunlight a day. Be sure there is enough room for a 6-inch (15 cm) space between the tree or shrub and the wall to allow for air circulation.

❦ Walls and other solid surfaces should be of unpainted wood, stone, stucco, brick or other maintenance-free material, and be at least 7 feet (180 cm) high and 10 feet (3 m) wide. Heat-reflecting, south-facing walls are good in areas where summers are cool. Open fences, trellises, lattice or free-standing supports are recommended where summers are hot.

❦ Decide on the type of shrub or tree you want. One- or two-year-old dwarf apple or pear trees are good choices if you are starting from scratch, and some nurseries carry small trees that have been espalier-trained. It is much more difficult to espalier an older specimen, so it is important to start training branches as early as possible.

What supports do I need?

Espalier needs sturdy support even when it is trained on a fence, lattice or wall.

❦ Supports, placed between the wall and the plant, are usually made of horizontal strands of 12- to 14-gauge wire stretched between two braced posts set firmly in the ground about 6 inches (15 cm) from the wall (see Diagram 1, p. 65).

❦ The lowest wire should be at least 18 inches (45 cm) above the ground and the top one no less than 6 inches below the top of the wall or solid fence.

❦ The others should be 12 to 24 inches (30 to 60 cm) apart, the number and placement depending on the size of the area to be covered and the shape chosen.

What about shape?

Although espaliered trees can be grown in a variety of patterns limited only by the imagination and the degree of skill, simple designs are easier to develop and maintain.

🌺 For single trees, try variations on the cordon design, which can be as simple as a single vertical branch or several branches trained horizontally (see diagrams, opposite).

🌺 The Belgian fence pattern (a lattice-work of branches) requires several trees but is both dramatic and effective for growing fruit because it provides cross-pollination, producing more fruit in a tiny space.

The side wall of a garage has been artfully incorporated into the garden by making it the backdrop for an ingenious tapestry of plants — an espaliered pear, trained into a fan shape, and the lush foliage of vines. A bit of trellis trickery creates a trompe l'oeil inset for a pair of matching terra-cotta urns.

HOW TO TRAIN HORIZONTAL ESPALIER

I At planting time, prepare the hole in the usual way and place the young tree midway between the posts. Cut it back to just above the bottom wire. Make sure there are at least three buds left to send out shoots.

2 Let three shoots grow, removing any others. Train the three shoots by lashing them to stakes of bamboo or other wood. Fasten the stakes to the wire support to keep the middle, leader branch vertical and the two laterals at a 45° angle during the first growing season.

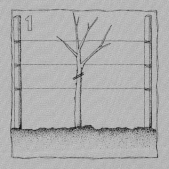

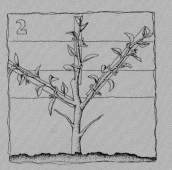

3 The first fall, after growth has stopped, lower the side shoots to a horizontal position and lash them to the lowest wire. This will slow their growth. Cut off the leader above the second wire. Continue to cut off new shoots that are not

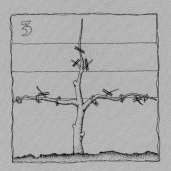

part of the pattern. The next spring, allow two more side shoots to grow horizontally and train them to the middle wire.

4 Pinch out the leader when the shape is completed, and keep arms trimmed to the desired length. Remove all flowers the first season and remove young fruit in subsequent seasons until the tree achieves its final shape.

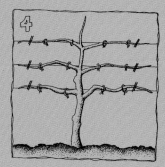

5 As soon as each branch of the espalier is established (the lowest tier is ready after the first season in the pattern described above), trim shoots to encourage the development of permanent fruiting spurs rather than vegetative growth. When trimming unwanted shoots from an established espalier branch, leave four or five buds. After the buds have started to grow, remove those nearest the end, leaving the fatter buds nearer the branch. They will develop into permanent fruiting spurs which will produce flowers and bear fruit year after year.

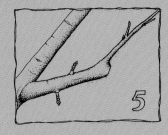

Flower Power

Although flowers most often take center stage with their eye-catching color and blooms, much of their impact depends on proper placement.

Just as trees or shrubs lend weight, scale and balance to the landscape, flowers also have qualities that contribute to the architecture of a garden. Yucca and euphorbia, for example, are strongly structural, whereas irises make a softer vertical statement. A feathery grouping of astilbe, with its plume-like flowers, is an ideal foil for more solid plants such as *Sedum spectabile*, while low plants like lamb's-ears (*Stachys byzantina*) and lady's-mantle (*Alchemilla mollis*) offer a different texture at the front of a mixed border or spilling onto a hard surface.

❧ It's a good idea to stick to one or two plants that will visually dominate and unify the garden, and provide a common element with which other plant materials are displayed.

❧ Another approach is to choose a theme — such as color — and use plants that bloom in various shades of that color and have foliage of differing size, shape and hue. For good color balance, avoid clashing tones, such as peach-pink flowers in a rose-pink border.

❧ Once you've settled on the flowers that will give the landscape its dramatic display, remember that a garden needs quiet passages, too. Otherwise, you'll end up with a chaos of colors. A stretch of grey-toned lamb's-ears or artemisia sets off poppies and peonies. A cloud of delicate white baby's-breath cools the little flames of red bergamot. Even a burst of green foliage provides a breathing space between brilliantly colored flowers.

❧ While deciding what works best in your garden, visit nurseries and move pots of plants around, if necessary, to see how they look together. And don't overlook the lessons you can learn from other gardens. Take photographs and make notes of good plant compositions when you see them.

❧ Finally, remember that less is definitely more. Use several of one variety of plant rather than one of several, and leave some margin for refining the details.

❧ If you keep all of this in mind, you'll be rewarded with a delightfully balanced garden that has been created by wise planning rather than promiscuous planting.

Drifts of breathtaking blue and white hydrangeas (right) define the curved edges of a grassy pathway that meanders through a Vancouver garden. In this case, a large grouping of a single plant in the same color is much more striking than a border of mixed flowers.

FLOWER INSETS

Even the tiniest flowers can make a strong color statement in the garden if you mass them for effect, and plant them for contrast. Dainty purple bellflowers (*Campanula portenschlagiana*) embroider a rugged stone wall (above), softening and enlivening the massiveness of the rock.

❧ Creeping rock plants probe deep into fissures, then stretch flat over the surrounding rock. It's easiest to set them in place while the wall is being built, leaving spaces just large enough to hold the plants.

❧ To plant them in an existing wall, wash loose earth off roots and wrap them in wet sphagnum moss (available at florists and nurseries), tie lightly with string, soak in a plant starter solution and chink them into the wall with a stick or the handle of a wooden spoon.

GARDEN *on a* WALL

Rather than relying on vines or climbers to camouflage a useful but less-than-perfect shed, an imaginative gardener has used the barn boards (left) as a backdrop for a display of folk-art plates and a decorative planting of flowers. A colorful mass of purple petunias draws the eye away from the shed and helps blend the structure into the garden setting.

PRETTY in PINK

The owner of this striking front garden in Vancouver has chosen a single-color theme for her plantings, balancing the different sizes, shapes and hues of pink flowers to very pleasing effect. Tall Japanese iris (*I. ensata*), with its elegant spiky foliage, is the focal point of the planting. From there, the eye moves to the graceful wash of pink lacecap hydrangea at right, its generous deep green leaves contrasting with the lighter green foliage of the surrounding plants. Delicate fuchsia in a hanging basket by the wood-shingled wall and a backdrop of multi-hued roses offer more variations on the pink theme. Hardy geranium, thyme and low-to-the-ground strawberry plants edge the garden, spilling gently onto the rose-colored brick drive.

THE TROPICAL SPLENDOR of CANNA

With its lily-like flowers and banana-leaf foliage, the exotic canna adds a touch of the tropics to any garden.

🌿 Unlike the larger varieties made popular years ago in park and estate plantings, today's smaller plants are in scale with almost any setting.

🌿 These modern hybrids come in a range of sizes and bloom in tones of red, orange, salmon and yellow. Some have glowing bronze foliage, making them highly ornamental even when they're not in bloom.

🌿 The bold canna needs thoughtful placement. A group of one color backed by shrubs and trees makes a strong statement. A group can also be used as the centerpiece of a formal island bed. Tall varieties make a good screen for a patio or utility area, while clumps of shorter ones are attractive among rocks or near steps.

🌿 Although cannas are perennials in Zones 8 to 10, most Canadian gardeners treat them as annuals, storing the rhizomes over winter.

🌿 Start cannas indoors in March by planting rhizomes 3 inches (7 cm) deep in a soilless mix or in pasteurized soil. Transplant to larger pots as plants become rootbound.

🌿 Harden off plants in late April and set in the ground when the soil temperature is about 15°C (60°F). Add a handful of balanced fertilizer when planting. Fertilize every two weeks and water during dry spells.

🌿 After the first frost kills the stems, dig up the rhizomes and dry them in a warm spot for a few days before storing in vermiculite.

Grey Matters

G rey is one of the most subtle yet effective of all colors in a planting scheme. It acts as a foil for other colors, making strong ones more vibrant and pales ones brighter. At the same time, grey itself can appear lighter or darker, depending on what is planted close to it. The peacekeeper in a planting scheme, it creates a quiet passage between otherwise disharmonious colors.

❧ As with any color, there are shades of grey, from light-reflecting silver to dull pewter. The grey effect of some plants is mostly a result of the texture of their leaves. Many are covered with soft hairs that deflect the light; under the hairs, the leaves may actually be green. The downy hairs protect the leaves from sunlight and reduce evaporation — a survival technique, since most grey plants originated in hot climates.

❧ A grey look can also be temporary, as is the case with silver sage (*Salvia argentea*). In its first year, leaf hairs are long and the plant looks pale grey, almost white. When it starts to bloom with whorls of pale yellow flowers on tall branching stems, it loses its grey look and becomes dark green.

❧ Grey can be effective on its own, especially in large specimen plants such as thistles and mulleins. In a group setting, pair it with plants whose leaves reflect blue tones — such as caryopteris, iris and bridalwreath spirea (*Spiraea* X *vanhouttei*) — rather than yellow ones.

The dimunitive rosy blooms and velvety grey leaves of lamb's-ears (*Stachys byzantina*) enhance a planting of delicate Persian cornflower (*Centaurea dealbata* 'Rosea').

The imposing biennial Scotch thistle (*Onopordum acanthium*) holds court by a latticed fence. Rosettes of furry grey leaves the first year give way to large velvety grey leaves the following year. Because of its height, it might need staking.

Lacy Japanese painted fern (*Athyrium nipponicum* 'Pictum') shines as a silver accent in a foliage garden.

The finely etched silver leaves of artemisia (far left) provide a striking border for blue globe thistle (*Echinops ritro*).

LAMB'S-EARS *are a* DELIGHT

There is nothing more charming or soothing in a brightly flowered border than a drift of soft lamb's-ears (*Stachys byzantina*).

❧ The plant's common name suits it well, since the thick, velvety elliptical leaves really do look like the ears of baby lambs. What makes this perennial so appealing, however, is its lovely soft-grey color, with an underlying hint of sea green.

❧ Lamb's-ears looks best next to glossy, deep greens or soft pinks and lavenders; its cool, subtle tones are lost when paired with raging oranges or brassy yellows. In the herb garden, pair it with curly or flat-leaved parsley. In the perennial garden, place it next to salmon-pink *Geranium endressii* 'Wargrave Pink' or pink creeping baby's-breath. The bright blue of veronica or catmint (*Nepeta* spp.) also makes a pleasing contrast.

❧ Hardy to Zone 4, lamb's-ears spreads quickly into a thick mat and flowers in mid-summer: felty spikes with sparse purplish-pink blooms rise about a foot above the 6-inch (15 cm) leaves.

❧ Like most grey-leaved plants, lamb's-ears needs sun, well-drained, lean soil and little water. Plants sometimes rot in hot, humid weather, but are otherwise trouble-free. Started plants are available at most nurseries.

CHAPTER SIX

CONTAINER GARDENING

*Plants in containers are
the free spirits of a garden. We can place them where
we like, plant them as we please, move them on a whim
and replant them as they fade. Portable and extremely
versatile, they offer an easy solution to dozens of outdoor
design dilemmas, both large and small. Best of all,
they allow us to garden beyond the restrictions
of climate, soil and season.*

Creating *a* Portable Garden

Container gardening lets us stretch the limits of nature to grow flowers, vegetables or herbs we might otherwise only dream of.

Take a pot or two, add soil, tuck in some lovely blooms or a sprinkling of seeds and presto! — you've created a portable garden. Believe it or not, container gardening is almost as easy as that. There are a few things you need to know before you start but once you have the basics in hand, you're ready to enjoy the almost instant pleasure of growing plants in pots.

The Container

❦ Before choosing a container, consider how the plant will grow — upright or trailing, bushy or tall and lean — and how big it will get. Proportions between plant and container are an important consideration, too. As a guideline, plants should be no higher than twice the height of the pot, and no more than half as wide again as the width of the container.

❦ Although you can never go wrong with terra-cotta pots and wooden planter boxes, don't be afraid to let your imagination (and your personality!) take flight in the garden. Found objects, such as painted or rubbed wicker baskets, kettles and other household castoffs, flue tiles, wooden crates and bushel baskets, make some of the most interesting and colorful containers for miniature gardens.

❦ Whatever containers you choose, remember that they should be in keeping with their surroundings. This applies to scale as well as type. Choose pots that are big enough (most people err on the side of insignificance) and vary the shapes and sizes within a grouping for greater effect.

❦ Don't overlook the possibilities of the empty vessel. A single unplanted clay urn, tall and imposing or rounded and oversize, can be a dramatic textural and sculptural contrast in a bed of low, mounding annuals.

Before You Plant

❦ Soil is surprisingly heavy so be sure that your balcony, railing or windowsill will support the weight of filled containers.

❦ Think carefully about positioning *before* you fill planters. Most large filled containers are too heavy to be moved without the help of rollers or a strong-armed friend.

❦ Since good drainage is essential in container gardening, make sure all your containers have drainage holes and enough outside clearance to drain properly. To prevent holes from clogging, cover the bottom with landscape fabric or fine screening.

❦ Soil also plays a critical role in proper drainage. Even the best earth from your garden is not porous enough for the restricted conditions of a container; use commercial growers' mix instead.

What to Plant

❦ Dwarf trees and shrubs, vines, annuals and perennials, vegetables and herbs — almost anything will grow in a container, given the right conditions. Local nurseries or garden centers are a good place to pick up ideas as well as growing information on a wide range of plants.

❦ You can also focus specifically on color (combining plants of the same color in different shapes, sizes and varieties) or on texture (combining the small, feathery leaves of one plant with the delicate blooms of another).

Care and Watering

❦ Once plants have used up the original nutrients in the soil (usually within a month, depending on the size of the container), you will need to add a liquid or water-soluble fertilizer twice a month.

❦ Most container gardens need daily watering; in hot weather, water smaller containers twice a day.

❦ To help reduce moisture loss, add surface mulch to containers or group several plants together in the same pot.

❦ Where possible, place containers near walls, fences and other sheltered spots in the garden for protection from wind, rain and constant sun. Since the temperature in protected spots is usually a few degrees warmer than in exposed areas, this is the best place for tender plants or for varieties that don't usually thrive in your growing zone.

❦ In early winter, empty small containers and bring indoors. For larger or permanent planters made of terra cotta or other porous material, remove or loosen soil, then cover containers to prevent damage and cracking from freezing and thawing. Metal or wooden containers can remain in the garden; just loosen the soil. Add twigs or boughs for winter interest.

INSTANT ANTIQUITY

A weathered look enhances most containers, especially those made of stone or terra cotta. Here's how to give new ones an air of antiquity — almost instantly!

❧ Prepare the pots by painting some live cultured yogurt (available in the dairy section of supermarkets) onto the pot surface and let dry. Terra cotta is very porous and will absorb the moisture quickly; stone pots may take a few days to dry out.

❧ Leave the prepared pots out in the sun. The salts in the clay of the pot will slowly leach out, leaving behind a delicate white patina.

FOR A MOSS-COVERED LOOK
❧ Gather moss spores when they mature in August. Put them in a blender, along with an equal amount of buttermilk; blend until the mixture is the consistency of white craft glue.

❧ Paint the surface of the pots with the mixture, then cover the prepared pots and set outside in a shady spot. Keep the covered surface moist to promote spore germination.

❧ In a month or so, delicate green moss will cover the once-new pots.

FOUND OBJECTS

With just a little imagination, the most unlikely objects can be transformed into tiny, perfect gardens. A massive hollowed-out rock (above), in the same shade and style as the surrounding flagstone patio, holds a lush planting of impatiens. A large cast-iron pot (below), filled with cheerful violas, enlivens the corner of a gravelled bed.

BONSAI: BEAUTY *in* MINIATURE

The goal of the ancient Japanese art of bonsai (literally, "tray planting") is to replicate in miniature a tree battered by strong winds, high altitude or poor soil. Careful pruning of branches, shoots, foliage and roots determines the form of the tree.

❧ Start a bonsai with an established nursery seedling hardy to your area. Trees with naturally small leaves, needles, flowers or fruit are good choices.

❧ Prune off some of the largest roots, leaving the fibrous ones. For good drainage, plant in light, granular soil.

❧ Feed young plants with a weak solution of fertilizer through spring and summer only, and not right after pruning. Consult books on bonsai for subsequent pruning.

❧ For the winter in mild, temperate parts of the country only, sink the pots in the garden to soil level, and protect plants with a layer of leaves. If necessary, prune roots and repot in early March. In colder areas, winter over the bonsai in an unheated sunroom.

On the upper terrace of a Vancouver garden, a stepped platform sheltered under a spreading cherry tree serves as the stage for a breathtaking bonsai collection.

The Pleasures *of a* Window-box Garden

Part house decoration, part container garden, window boxes are enjoying a colorful revival across the country.

Never out of fashion in Europe and in many rural areas of North America, window boxes filled with seasonal blooms create a visual link between house and landscape and enliven even the barest architectural structure. Best of all, they provide a sheltered growing space for an amazing array of plants which often last far past the first frosted days of autumn. Here's how to get the most out of a windowful of flowers.

❧ Choose a window that offers a pleasing face to the outside world and allows the addition of a window box without damage or complicated construction. Most window boxes can be attached to the framework of a window with screws or mounted on brackets directly below the windowsill.

❧ Make sure you can tend the box from inside the house or reach it easily from the outside without having to trample through

flowerbeds or climb ladders.

❧ Window boxes come in a variety of materials, but the most common are wood and plastic. Line wooden boxes with plastic before planting to help retain water.

❧ Terra-cotta planters are heavier and more porous and so require more work to mount and more effort to maintain. Their weight when planted also limits use on many house windows unless they are mounted very securely.

❧ Whatever window box you select, make sure it is in keeping with the style and color of your house — and in proportion to the size of the window. As a rule, boxes should be as long as the window is wide, and at least 6 inches (15 cm) wide and deep.

❧ Because window boxes are directly attached to the house and form part of its ornamentation, they look best when they are in constant bloom from spring until fall. This is one reason why long-flowering plants such

as geraniums and impatiens are such popular window-box choices.

❧ Select plants to suit the location of your window boxes and remember to take into account the effects of hot sun, less rain (if the window is sheltered by roof or eaves) and exposure to wind.

❧ Combinations of small plants, both upright and trailing, are most effective. Among the most popular are ivy geraniums, lobelia, begonias, petunias, pansies and dwarf zinnias. You can limit your planting scheme to one color or experiment with contrasting colors, adding variegated foliage for interest and texture.

From a striking planting of dwarf zinnias and English ivy (far left) to a cascade of miniature blooms (right), window-box gardens add color and charm to any house.

VARIATIONS
on a THEME

Imaginative plantings
turn a simple wooden
barrel into a container
garden. For a variety of
looks, change the
plantings with the
seasons.

❧ Bold white cottage
tulips (top left) against a
flowering azalea trumpet
the arrival of spring.

❧ Turn a barrel into a
miniature water garden
(top right) by lining it
with plastic or a pond
liner. This one holds
water hyacinths and
sedge.

❧ A tumble of bright
annuals (bottom left)
captures the glory days of
summer. Purple fan
flower (*Scaevola aemula*)
and golden creeping
zinnia (*Sanvitalia
procumbens*) border taller
plantings of scarlet
zinnias, purple heliotrope
and yellow marigolds.

❧ Chrysanthemums and
ornamental kale (bottom
right) celebrate the
colors of autumn.

ELEGANT ACCENTS

I n keeping with the pristine formality of a delightful
Victorian garden (right) in downtown Toronto, an
ornate white stone planter holds a standard fuchsia —
a lovely accent against the soft grey facade of the
backyard shed with its decorative period mouldings.
A graceful stone column (above) lends an air of
antiquity to a pretty summer garden and holds a
container lushly planted with pink impatiens and
delicate night-scented stock. The owner has successfully
balanced the fullness of the container plantings with
the proportions of the column.

CONTAINER VINES

Here's a delightful new take on the classic charm of a vine-covered front entrance. Decorative terra-cotta planters (opposite page) hold a topiary of English ivy, trained on wire forms into miniature wreaths.

Definitely a classy way to say welcome! Intricate cones of twigs (left), inserted in large stone pots, provide a base for climbing sweet-peas. With time, this annual vine will completely cover the cones and create a striking sculpture of blooms on either side of the front door.

POOLSIDE PANACHE

Plants in containers are one of the prettiest ways to dress up a poolside patio (above). A cerise standard bougainvillea is surrounded by pots of petunias (not yet in bloom) and containers of cerise and pink impatiens.

BLACK-EYED SUSAN VINE

If a pot of geraniums on the patio has become a bit ho-hum, it's time you discovered the black-eyed Susan vine (*Thunbergia alata*) — fast-growing yet dainty, colorful but not brash, equally at home twining over the handle of a twig basket filled with marigolds or adding a splash of color to a muted container of hostas. Neat in habit, it needs no deadheading and flowers until frost.

❧ Thunbergia is charming in window boxes or complementing the warm tones of a terra-cotta pot, but a formal arrangement of two large urns flanking a garden gate can also be striking. Turn a tomato cage upside down over the urn and bury the top rung; wire together the prongs at the top to form an obelisk. Plant thunbergia seedlings around the perimeter and train the vines to cover the wires.

❧ This cheerful vine grows to about 4 feet (120 cm) under ideal conditions and has a profusion of simple black-throated orange flowers about 1 inch (2.5 cm) across; its arrow-shape leaves are medium green. 'Suzie Mixed' also includes buff, pale orange and yellow flowers, some without black throats.

❧ Give seeds a head start indoors under lights six to eight weeks before the last frost. Plant two or three seeds to a pot and pinch out all but one seedling. Insert a small stake in each pot to support the seedlings or they'll tangle.

❧ Pinch out the growing tip when the vines are about four inches (10 cm) long to promote side branching. Feed weekly with a diluted balanced fertilizer once the seedlings are up and growing.

❧ Although vigorous, thunbergia is sensitive to temperature extremes. Harden off seedlings before planting outside and shelter from cool nights. Grow in sun or semi-shade, keep well watered and fertilized — and enjoy their sunny disposition!

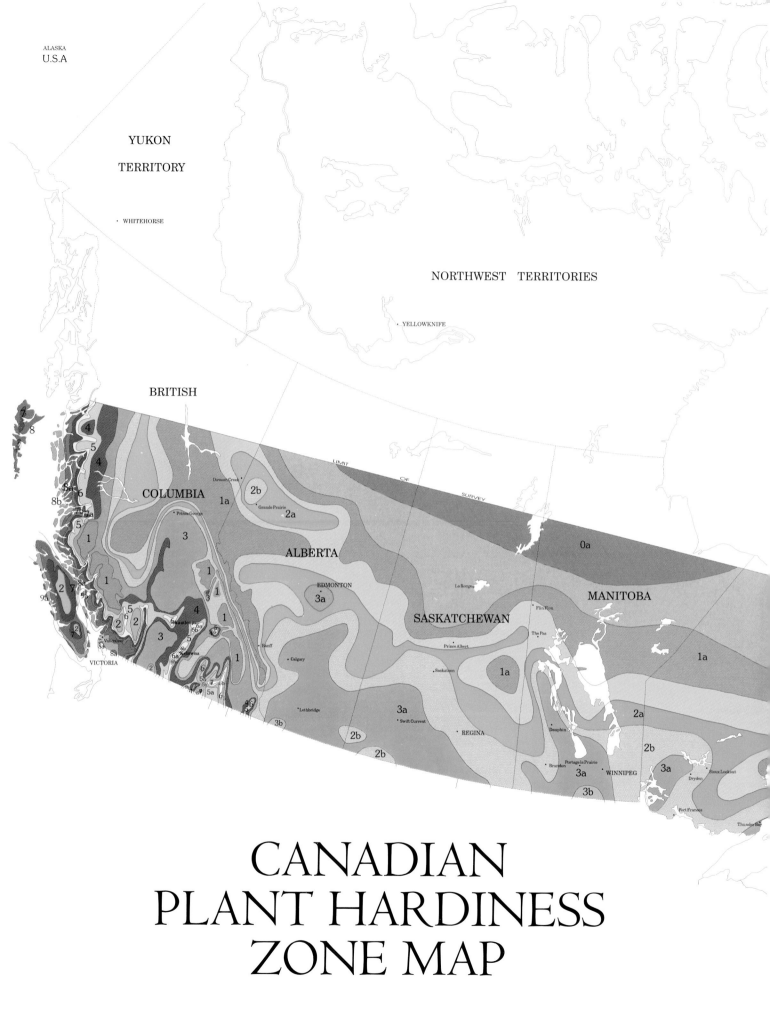

CANADIAN
PLANT HARDINESS
ZONE MAP

This map shows the areas of winter hardiness for ornamental plants in the more heavily populated areas of Canada. The map is based on a formula that takes into consideration several meteorological factors affecting the hardiness of a plant in a given location.

❧ The most important element in plant survival is the minimum temperature during the winter. Other important considerations are the length of the frost-free period, summer rainfall, maximum temperatures, snow cover and wind.

❧ The hardiness areas have been divided into 10 zones. The one marked 0 is the coldest. Other zones are progressively milder, to 9, which is the mildest. A given zone on this map corresponds only approximately to a zone of the same number in the United States Department of Agriculture Plant Hardiness Zone Map, which has been in use in Canada for a number of years. This present map, however, presents more detail for Canada.

❧ If data warranted it, each zone has been subdivided into a dark and a light section to represent, respectively, the colder and milder portions of the zone. If undivided, the zone was designated by the color of the colder section.

LABRADOR

QUEBEC

SURVEY

OF

LIMIT

Gagnon

NEWFOUNDLAND

4b

Gander

ST. JOHN'S

3b

Corner Brook

5a

5b

5b

6a

0b

Baie Comeau

Chibougamau

5a

P.E.I.

6a

CHARLOTTETOWN

5a

Sydney

1b

2

Campbellton

NEW

BRUNSWICK

3a

NTARIO

3b

Edmundston

Moncton

NOVA

SCOTIA

1a

4a

FREDERICTON

5b

5a

QUEBEC

Timmins

Noranda

5a

St. John

HALIFAX

1b

3a

Trois Rivières

6a

Superior

Sudbury

Montreal

Yarmouth

6b

Sault Ste. Marie

OTTAWA

5a

4b

Kingston

Lake Huron

Barrie

5b

4b

Lake Ontario

TORONTO

7a

6a

London

6b

Lake
Michigan

Windsor

7a

Lake
Erie

7b

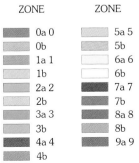

LEGEND

NOTE: Darker tint indicates colder part, lighter tint of same color indicates milder part.

ZONE	ZONE
0a 0	5a 5
0b	5b
1a 1	6a 6
1b	6b
2a 2	7a 7
2b	7b
3a 3	8a 8
3b	8b
4a 4	9a 9
4b	

CANADIAN PLANT HARDINESS ZONES

Agriculture Canada's Plant Hardiness Zone map (reproduced on previous page) is still the most relevant source of climate information for Canadian gardeners. And even though it was compiled in 1987, it will remain current until there is a change in Canada's climate. The majority of Canadian nurseries rely on it for their selection of hardy regional plants, trees and shrubs.

❧ Small areas with peculiar microclimates often exist within a zone. These areas are colder or milder than the surrounding area. They are usually too small to locate on the hardiness map or they may not have been recorded. In addition, sharp changes in elevation, as found in mountainous or hilly regions, cause a difference in climate that cannot be accurately indicated on the map.

❧ The user should also remember that the zone lines are arbitrarily drawn and that the zones merge gradually into each other. Consequently, conditions near the border of one zone may closely approximate those of an adjacent zone.

Spring *and* Fall Frost Dates

Environment Canada's spring and fall frost dates are based on minimum temperatures recorded every day at the 2,500 climate stations across Canada. The dates of the last spring and fall frosts are recorded over a 30-year period. Although Mother Nature doesn't follow the chart exactly, you can use these frost dates to gauge when it's safe to plant tender annuals in the spring and when to harvest cold-sensitive crops in the fall.

STATION	LAST SPRING FROST	FIRST FALL FROST
BRITISH COLUMBIA		
Chilliwack	Apr 6	Nov 9
Dawson Creek	Jun 5	Aug 29
Kamloops	May 1	Oct 5
Kelowna	May 19	Sep 20
Nanaimo	Apr 28	Oct 17
Port Alberni	May 8	Oct 15
Prince George	Jun 4	Sep 3
Terrace	May 5	Oct 17
Vancouver	Mar 28	Nov 5
Vernon	Apr 29	Oct 4
Victoria	Apr 19	Nov 5

STATION	LAST SPRING FROST	FIRST FALL FROST
NWT AND YUKON		
Whitehorse	Jun 11	Aug 25
Yellowknife	May 27	Sep 15
ALBERTA		
Athabaska	Jun 1	Aug 29
Calgary	May 23	Sep 15
Edmonton	May 7	Sep 23
Grande Prairie	May 18	Sep 13
Lethbridge	May 17	Sep 18
Medicine Hat	May 16	Sep 22
Red Deer	May 25	Sep 9
SASKATCHEWAN		
Moose Jaw	May 20	Sep 18
Prince Albert	Jun 2	Sep 4
Regina	May 21	Sep 10
Saskatoon	May 21	Sep 15
Weyburn	May 22	Sep 12
MANITOBA		
Brandon	May 27	Sep 10
The Pas	May 27	Sep 17
Thompson	Jun 15	Aug 16
Winnipeg	May 25	Sep 22

HARDY PERENNIALS

Perennial borders in Zones 2 and 3 can be just as floriferous and varied as those grown in warmer zones. Here's our pick of cold-climate flowers with iron-clad constitutions and long-lasting blooms.

Adonis vernalis (spring adonis)
❦ low growing, with yellow flowers that bloom in spring

Artemisia stellerina 'Silver Brocade'
❦ silver-grey foliage

Aurinia saxatilis (basket-of-gold, perennial alyssum)
❦ yellow flowers that bloom in spring

Bergenia cordifolia (bergenia, giant rockfoil)
❦ large, attractive leaves and pink flowers that bloom in spring

Campanula cochleariifolia (creeping bellflower)
❦ dainty blue flowers that bloom early to mid-summer

Clematis integrifolia (solitary clematis)
❦ blue flowers that bloom early to mid-summer
❦ grows 2 to 3 feet (60 to 90 cm)

Dictamnus albus (gas plant)
❦ white or pink flowers that bloom early to mid-summer

Hemerocallis spp. (daylily)
❦ yellow, orange, red or pink flowers
❦ blooms in spring, summer or fall

Station	Last Spring Frost	First Fall Frost	Station	Last Spring Frost	First Fall Frost
ONTARIO			**NEW BRUNSWICK**		
Barrie	May 26	Sep 16	Bathurst	May 19	Sep 26
Hamilton	Apr 29	Oct 15	Edmundston	May 28	Sep 18
Kingston	May 2	Oct 10	Fredericton	May 20	Sep 22
London	May 9	Oct 8	Grand Falls	May 24	Sep 24
Ottawa	May 6	Oct 5	Moncton	May 24	Sep 27
Owen Sound	May 12	Oct 15	Saint John	May 18	Oct 4
Parry Sound	May 17	Sep 28			
Peterborough	May 18	Sep 20	**PRINCE EDWARD ISLAND**		
St. Catharines	May 2	Oct 17	Charlottetown	May 17	Oct 14
Sudbury	May 17	Sep 25	Summerside	May 9	Oct 19
Thunder Bay	Jun 1	Sep 15	Tignish	May 23	Oct 9
Timmins	Jun 8	Sep 6			
Toronto	May 9	Oct 6	**NOVA SCOTIA**		
Windsor	Apr 25	Oct 22	Halifax	May 6	Oct 20
			Kentville	May 16	Oct 5
QUEBEC			Shelburne	May 14	Sep 29
Baie Comeau	May 28	Sep 15	Sydney	May 24	Oct 13
Chicoutimi	May 17	Sep 30	Yarmouth	May 1	Oct 18
Montreal	May 3	Oct 7			
Quebec City	May 13	Sep 29	**NEWFOUNDLAND**		
Rimouski	May 13	Sep 30	Corner Brook	May 22	Oct 12
Sherbrooke	Jun 1	Sep 10	Grand Falls	Jun 2	Sep 26
Trois-Rivières	May 19	Sep 23	St. John's	Jun 2	Oct 12
Thetford Mines	May 28	Sep 14			

Monarda
> 'Marshall's Delight' (bee balm, bergamot)
> ❧ pink flowers that bloom in midsummer
> ❧ foliage resistant to mildew

Nepata X *ucranica*
> 'Dropmore' (catmint)
> ❧ purple or blue flowers that bloom in midsummer

Primula cortusoides
> (cortusa primrose)
> ❧ pink flowers that bloom in spring
> ❧ one of the hardier primroses

Pulmonaria saccharata
> (bethlehem sage)
> ❧ flowers bloom pink in the spring, then fade to purple or blue
> ❧ leaves are spotted with silver

Salvia X *superba*
> (violet sage)
> ❧ blue flowers that bloom in midsummer

Yucca glauca
> (small soapweed)
> ❧ sword-like foliage, with white flowers that bloom in midsummer

HARDY ROSES

These winter-hardy *Rosa* cultivars were bred by Agriculture Canada, and are resistant to blackspot and powdery mildew. All are hardy to Zones 2 or 3, and flower freely through summer (except where noted).

1. EXPLORER SERIES

Rugosa Shrub Type
❧ 'Martin Frobisher' - soft pink
  - 5 to 6-1/2 feet (1.5 to 2 m). Zone 2.
❧ 'Jens Munk' - medium pink
  - 5 to 6-1/2 feet (1.5 to 2 m). Zone 2.
❧ 'Henry Hudson' - white/pink
  - 20 to 27 inches (50 to 70 cm). Zone 2.
❧ 'David Thompson' - medium red
  - 48 inches (120 cm). Zone 2.
❧ 'Charles Albanel' - medium red
  - flowers repeatedly through early summer, sporadically in late summer
  - 20 inches (50 cm). Zone 2.

Kordesii Climber or Pillar Type
❧ 'John Davis' - medium pink
  - branches 6-1/2 to 8 feet (2 to 2.5 m). Zone 3.
❧ 'Captain Samuel Holland' - medium pink
  - branches 6 feet (180 cm). Zone 3.
❧ 'Louis Jolliet' - medium pink
  - branches 48 inches (120 cm). Zone 3.
(See page 10 for additional listings.)

Kordesii Shrub and Miscellaneous Types
❧ 'John Franklin' - medium red
  - 48 inches (120 cm). Zone 3.
❧ 'Champlain' - dark red
  - 40 inches (1 m). Zone 3.
❧ 'Alexander MacKenzie' - deep red
  - 5 to 6-1/2 feet (1.5 to 2 m). Zone 3b.

❧ 'Frontenac' - deep pink
  - peak bloom in June, continues to flower to end of September
  - 40 inches (1 m). Zone 3.
❧ 'Simon Fraser' - medium pink
  - 2 feet (60 cm). Zone 3.

2. PARKLAND SERIES

The cultivars in the Parkland series are all shrub roses and were developed using a native prairie rose species.

❧ 'Morden Blush'
  - light pink in cool temperatures, ivory or white in warm weather
  - 20 to 40 inches (50 cm to 1 m). Zone 2b.
❧ 'Morden Fireglow' - scarlet
  - 20 to 27 inches (50 to 70 cm). Zone 2b.
❧ 'Adelaide Hoodless' - red
  - flowers in June and July
  - 40 inches (1 m). Zone 2.
❧ 'Morden Amorette' - carmine to rose bengal
  - 12 to 20 inches (30 to 50 cm). Zone 3.
❧ 'Cuthbert Grant' - crimson
  - blooms in June and July
  - 30 to 40 inches (80 cm to 1 m). Zone 3.
❧ 'Morden Centennial' - medium pink
  - flowers mostly in June, August and September
  - 27 to 40 inches (70 cm to 1 m). Zone 2.

- 'Morden Cardinette' - cardinal red
  - 12 to 20 inches (30 to 50 cm).
  Zone 3b.
- 'Morden Ruby' - ruby red
  - 40 inches (1 m). Zone 2.
- 'Winnipeg Parks' - medium red
  - 15 to 27 inches (40 to 70 cm).
  Zone 2b.

3. OTHER HARDY ROSES

As well as the many Canadian-bred roses listed above, several popular old-fashioned shrub roses with fragrant double blooms also do well in Zones 2 and 3. Most bloom heavily just once, usually in June. Species with hardy cultivars to consider include *Rosa blanda, R. glauca, R. nitida, R. rugosa, R. spinosissima* and *R. suffulta*.

FALL GARDEN WRAP-UP

Here's what to do in the fall to get the most out of your garden next spring.

Bulbs

Tender summer bulbs should be lifted and stored indoors after the first light frost.

- Remove excess soil from the roots of dahlias, gladiolus and begonias, and cut stems to 2 inches (5 cm).
- Store glads in open cardboard boxes in a dry, cool location. Pack other bulbs and corms in slightly moist peat moss or sawdust and store at 40°F (5°C).

Annuals

Propagate summer annuals now to save money next spring.

- Cuttings taken from geraniums, impatiens, begonias and other annuals will easily root, and can be overwintered under a light or on a windowsill. Root more cuttings during winter.

Perennials

Dividing is necessary for the continued health of perennials. When they're crowded or overgrown, they bloom less

profusely, and early fall is a good time to rejuvenate them.

- Gently divide them with a garden fork and replant only a few of the best sections. Share the rest with a neighbor. Don't forget to cover the new transplants with a mulch during winter.

Roses

Roses need winter protection. Various methods can be used to insulate the roots and bud union — plastic rose collars, newspaper cones, or garden soil.

- Trim plants back to 18 inches (45 cm) and protect the bottom 12 inches (30 cm).
- Evergreen boughs placed over the roses in January collect the snow and provide even more insulation. Good snow cover is nature's way of protecting plants.
- Delay final pruning until spring.

Grass

Grass seed planted in the fall is especially successful. The cooler nights, warm soil and moisture

favor quick germination and growth to a size that will successfully survive over the winter.

- Level the area, adding sterilized topsoil where necessary. Evenly broadcast premium-grade seed and lightly cover it by raking with a leaf rake.
- Water well each day if the weather is dry until most seed has germinated.
- Avoid walking on the new lawn until it's time for the first mowing (when the seedlings have reached a height one-third higher than your regular mowing height).
- Don't apply fertilizer or herbicides until next spring.

Tools

Storing gardening tools and equipment is the last task before the garden is put to bed for the winter.

- Clean and sharpen tools for a head start in spring. A light coating of oil will prevent rust and prolong the life of your tools.

THE CONTRIBUTORS

LIZ PRIMEAU is the editor of *Canadian Gardening*. In her five years with the magazine, she has visited gardens in all parts of Canada and has heard firsthand from committed Canadian gardeners about what works — or doesn't work! — in this widely varied climate of ours. An avid and experienced gardener herself, she has also been a featured speaker at gardening conferences, trade shows and garden clubs. Liz Primeau writes regularly on gardening for *The Globe and Mail's* Design section, and has also worked as a writer and editor with *Weekend Magazine*, *Toronto Life*, *Chatelaine*, *City Woman*, *Vista* and *Ontario Living* during a 23-year journalistic career.

PENNY ARTHURS is a widely respected garden designer and the owner of her own design company, The Chelsea Gardener. She has designed city and country gardens in and around Toronto and across the country — many of which are featured on annual garden tours. A graduate of The English Gardening School, one of England's leading schools of garden design, Penny Arthurs writes regularly on garden design for *Canadian Gardening* and other magazines, and has also lectured and made television appearances on the subject.

FRANK KERSHAW has taught gardening courses at the Civic Garden Center in Toronto and at the Royal Botanical Gardens in Hamilton, Ontario, and has lectured widely on gardening topics in Canada, the United States and in other countries. Over the last ten years, he has led numerous garden tours, and has visited and photographed over 300 gardens in North America, the Caribbean and Europe. Frank Kershaw is director of planning, research and construction for the Metropolitan Toronto Parks and Culture Department which administers some 4600 hectares of regional open space.

Photographers

DAN CALLIS: page 82.

CANAPRESS/ McEVOY: pages 37 (middle), 80 (bottom right).

ALAIN CHAREST: pages 58, 71 (left).

EWEN COXSWORTH: page 59 (bottom).

CHRISTOPHER DEW: pages 3, 6, 10, 14 (top), 21, 24, 29 (bottom), 30, 34, 36, 44 (top), 47, 50, 72, 76 (bottom), 81 (top), 83 (left).

TURID FORSYTH: pages 46 (middle), 74.

WILLIAM HART: page 49 (top right and bottom left).

LINDA HINK: pages 59 (top), 83 (bottom).

JIM HODGINS: page 37 (bottom).

FRANK KERSHAW: pages 9, 11, 12 (inset), 13, 14 (inset and bottom), 15, 17 (inset), 23, 26, 37 (top), 38 (bottom), 39, 43 (top), 45 (middle), 46 (top and bottom), 48, 49 (top left), 54, 55, 57, 60 (bottom), 61, 64, 80 (top and bottom right),

BERT KLASSEN: pages 5 (photo of Liz Primeau), 12 (top), 22, 25 (top), 27, 31, 33, 35, 38 (top), 42, 43 (bottom left), 44 (inset), 45 (bottom), 49 (bottom right), 71 (right), 73, 78, 79 (top left), 81 (bottom), 83 (top right).

CLAUDE NOEL:
pages 8, 16.

JERRY SHULMAN:
pages 1 (detail), 12
(bottom), 28, 41, 45
(top), 52, 60 (top),
66 (left), 68, 70, 79
(bottom left and
right).

DAVID
TOMLINSON:
pages 62, 76 (top).

PADDY WALES:
front cover; pages 1
(center), 4, 17 (right),
19, 20, 25 (bottom),
29 (top), 43 (bottom
right), 51, 53, 56, 66
(right), 67, 69, 77.

Illustrations on pages
18 and 65 by
BONNIE
SUMMERFELDT
BOISSEAU.

The map of Canada's Plant Hardiness Zones
(pages 84-85) was produced by the Centre for
Land and Biological Resources Research, Research
Branch, Agriculture Canada from information
supplied by the Ottawa Research Station and the
Meteorological Branch, Environment Canada 1993.

We would like to thank Bryan Monette and Ron
St. John of the Research Branch for their kind
help in supplying us with this material.

Acknowledgments

We are grateful to the many talented garden writers from across the country whose articles in *Canadian Gardening* magazine over the last six years have been an inspiration for this book series. These include Penny Arthurs, Alain Charest, Trevor and Brenda Cole, Janet Davis, Jane Giffen, Rebecca Hanes-Fox, Ross Hawthorne, Elizabeth Irving, Frank Kershaw, Laura Langston, Ann Rhodes, John Simkins, Anne Marie Van Nest, Andrew Vowles and Paddy Wales.

We are also indebted to the many Canadian gardeners from coast to coast who so generously shared their gardening successes with *Canadian Gardening* and provided the magazine with the wealth of stunning and inspirational photographs which appear throughout this book. Our thanks to Babs Brock, Terri and Peter Clark, Gunild Dutt, Sharon and Brian Edey, Doris Fancourt-Smith, Brian Folmer, Turid Forsyth, Laurie and Doreen Freeman, Michael Griffin, Sandy and Elena Heard, Linda Janzen, Audrey Litherland, Nancy and Ted Maitland, Jean McKay, Barry More, Rosemary Pauer, Valerie and Carl Pfeiffer, Nick and Wendy Seminchuk, David Tomlinson and Julie White. We would also like to thank Mrs. P. Vanneste, Kay Skeat and John H. Whitworth, Jr.

In some cases, it was not possible to identify gardens or their owners from the photographs of garden details which we also feature in this book. We acknowledge them here and are are grateful for the use of this material.

SPECIAL THANKS

This book could not have been published without the help of many people, and it is my pleasure to acknowledge them here. First, Wanda Nowakowska, Madison Press project editor: Wanda's vision, dedication and creativity are inherent to the book, and her patience and good humor made working with her a pleasure. Rebecca Hanes-Fox, *Canadian Gardening* managing editor, was an invaluable idea person as we worked out the original concept, and her professional editing and proofreading made the book's production flow smoothly. Gordon Sibley's elegant design and type choices give the book class, as do the photographs provided by many of the magazine's contributors. And along the way, even if we haven't said so, we have appreciated the support and advice of Tom Hopkins, the magazine's editorial director, and the commitment of the publisher, Phil Whalen.

— *Liz Primeau*

Selected Bibliography

Harris, Marjorie. *The Canadian Gardener.* Toronto: Random House of Canada Limited, 1990.

Hillier, Malcolm. *Container Gardening Through the Year.* Toronto: Little, Brown & Company (Canada) Limited, 1995.

McVicar, Jekka. *Jekka's Complete Herb Book.* London: Kyle Cathie Limited, 1994.

Osborne, Robert. *Roses for Canadian Gardens.* Toronto: Key Porter Books, 1991.

Waterhouse-Hayward, Alex. "Leaves much to be desired," in *Harrowsmith,* June 1993, pp. 88-98.

INDEX

EDITORIAL DIRECTOR Hugh Brewster

PROJECT EDITOR Wanda Nowakowska

EDITORIAL ASSISTANCE Rebecca Hanes-Fox

PRODUCTION DIRECTOR Susan Barrable

PRODUCTION COORDINATOR Sandra L. Hall

BOOK DESIGN AND LAYOUT Gordon Sibley Design Inc.

PRINTING AND BINDING Tien Wah Press

CANADIAN GARDENING'S
GREAT IDEAS *for the* GARDEN
was produced by
Madison Press Books